THE GIFT OF GOVERNMENT

In the quest to meet the summit of our potential, it is my firm conviction that our American Constitution will serve future generations with all of their complexities, as it has the current generation and the generations of our forebears.

RICHARD B. RUSSELL

THE RICHARD B. RUSSELL LECTURE SERIES

The Richard B. Russell Foundation and the University of Georgia have joined in establishing this lecture series to honor the late Senator Russell. The Richard B. Russell Lectures will extend through the 1980s, addressing the Bicentennial of the Federal Constitution and encompassing the Charter of the University of Georgia in 1785. The Russell Lectures are scheduled for each year during this decade, at which time a distinguished guest of the University of Georgia will present three addresses on some notable aspect of the Constitution.

THE GIFT OF GOVERNMENT

Political Responsibility from the English Restoration to American Independence

J. R. POLE

The Richard B. Russell Lectures
Number One

THE UNIVERSITY OF GEORGIA PRESS
Athens

Printed in the United States of America

Library of Congress Cataloging in Publication Data

Pole, J. R. (Jack Richon)
The gift of government.

(The Richard B. Russell lectures; no. 1)
Includes bibliographical references and
index.
1. Representative government and
representation—Great Britain—History.
2. Representative government and representation
—United States—History. I. Title.
II. Series.
JF1051.P58 1983   328'.3'09   82-13533
ISBN 0-8203-0652-5

For Vann Woodward

Contents

Preface

We live in a world dominated by a tumult of undigested and often indigestible news. Communication is one of our major industries. The media of communication have patently contributed to the idea that everyone is entitled to know anything that he or she wants to know. The mechanical aspects of this situation are a product of modern technological skill; but even the more political attributes of the rage for news can be considered, in true historical terms, comparatively modern. The political dimension most easily taken for granted lies in the public's right to know the details of legislative proceedings and votes and the corresponding obligation of both administrations and legislators to keep their constituents in frequent touch with their actions and to give convincing reasons for these actions.

This book, which took shape as a result of the invitation of President Fred C. Davison of the University of Georgia and of the Trustees of the Richard B. Russell Foundation to give three lectures on British and American constitutional ideas down to the American Revolution, is occupied with a different world, in which no one was considered to have a general right to information. Any such claim pertained to one's specific and legitimate interest in the subject under discussion. Political news stood in the relation of a ward of court. The right to govern was a gift of God. What courts and parliaments owed to the people was the gift of good government; but government itself, one might say, was too important a matter to be entrusted to the people.

The breakdown of this set of rules and conventions into the

more modern democratic idea that government derives its moral authority from its ability to satisfy the people, and the corresponding idea that the people's representatives owe them a form of instant accountability, is the history of a transformation of states of mind. Much of it can be studied formally within the confines of the history of certain famous representative institutions: the Parliament of Great Britain, the legislative assemblies of the American colonies, the American Continental Congress, the Congress of the United States. These institutions have had a profound continuity. And continuity is one of the most assuredly stabilizing influences in a world of violent political fluctuations frequently accompanied by social and economic disorder. These institutional continuities may in turn be given credit for a stabilizing effect on the minds of most of those who have worked within their orbit. Nevertheless, the changes that have taken place under this institutional cover have been profound changes, whose significance can be understood only by taking full account of the older world from which our modern one uneasily (at times unexpectedly) derives. It seems to be more than ever true that young students of history believe that all the history they really need to know is that which has occurred within their own lifetimes—or, at the most, those of their parents. They could not make a more profound mistake. If this book succeeds in revealing the depth of the contrast between the older and the modern style under the cover of the same or similar institutions, it will not have been useless as a contribution to historical understanding. It may even have contributed to the more modest ambition of getting a better comprehension of our own times.

For these reasons I hope it will appear as rather more than a mere footnote to the study of political representation which I unloaded on the world in the mid-1960s. That was a fertile period in the progress of the study of political ideas and their practical consequences. Since then, a great proportion of the new research in history has been directed to social networks and economic development. It would have been possible for a student undertaking his or her first research in the somewhat unharmonized excitement of these socioeconomic studies to get the idea that all this could have gone on without politics. The truth, however, is that the character of politics makes the difference between success and failure in other fields and that, in any case, the economic activities of a society, as well as its social structures, expectations, and sanctions, cannot be understood without entering into the politics of these things themselves.

For all these reasons I am grateful to the Trustees of the Richard B. Russell Foundation for honoring me with the invitation, which has given me the opportunity of bringing these ideas together and of launching what I am sure will be a very successful series of lectures. During the course of collecting information and seeking advice, I have collected obligations which it is a pleasure to mention. Jack P. Greene and Joyce Appleby read the manuscript of the lectures as originally delivered at the University of Georgia and made most valuable comments, which I hope have led to some improvement and clarification in this considerably revised and extended form of my text. John Walsh and Paul Langford interrupted their busy tutorial schedules to read and advise me, the first on the first chapter and the latter on the entire manuscript in its earlier form. The chapters on parliamentary and assembly reporting also gained from the comments of the history seminar at the Johns Hopkins University. Sheila Lambert was generous with her expertise on parliamentary procedure in the eighteenth century and Linda Colley with her knowledge of British opposition politics.

The long-distance researcher is liable to suffer from a particular form of intellectual loneliness. The work on this book has confirmed my longstanding opinion that, with all the help we obtain from film, there is no substitute for visiting libraries and archives in person. But I should like to thank Connie Schulz for her loyal and consistent help in answering inquiries, which always called for visits to the archive resources of the Washington area and for supplying much valuable information, often sharpened by her own perceptive comments. Sue Falb guided me to some of the problems of early Maryland. In addition, I have always been able to count on the help of the staffs of the Massachusetts Historical Society, the Historical Society of Pennsylvania (without whom I would probably not have discovered Mathew Carey's *Pennsylvania Evening Herald*), the Historical Society of Maryland, the Maryland Hall of Records, and, above all, the Rare Book Room of the Library of Congress. Back at home, Mary-Rose Murphy has conscientiously checked my references, and the staff of the Modern History Faculty typed the manuscript.

The American side of the work was also advanced during my tenure of a Guest Scholar's privileges at the Woodrow Wilson International Center for Scholars in the winter of 1978–79. It is a pleasure to thank James H. Billington and the staff of the Center for the great resources which they placed at my disposal in that productive six months.

During my stay in Athens, I was happy to enjoy the hospitality of the Honorable Robert G. Stephens and of Grace Stephens, to whom I record my warmest appreciation. Dean Rusk was one of the many whose kindness enhanced the pleasure of my visit, and I am grateful to him for introducing my lectures. And, finally, I want to thank those friends whose hospitality made it possible for me to spend many months in the Library of Congress and has made Washington a second home to me.

J. R. P.
St. Catherine's College
Oxford

24 May 1982

CHAPTER ONE

Political Authority from Divine Right to Utilitarianism

The Restoration of Charles II to the English throne in 1660 revealed the English people as a nation of monarchists. The restored monarchy itself had much to restore, the most important item being the fundamental connection between state and church. In its early years Charles's government was guided by two principles. The first was to secure the Church of England's undoubted supremacy, if necessary by driving the dissenting opposition underground. This, however, was at least as much the aim of the new Parliament as of the king himself and required the passage of several severely repressive acts against the freedom of dissenting movement and worship. Parliament made itself into an extremely active agent of policy. This parliamentary role therefore tends to obscure the second principle, which had to do with the sources of political authority. Militia acts passed in 1661 and 1662 gave the king direct control of all armed forces and relinquished any ghost of a claim by Parliament; a Triennial Act in 1661 declared that Parliament ought to meet every three years but did not revive the Long Parliament Act of 1641, which had provided for automatic elections and the assembling of both houses even if not ordered by the king. In other words, this was a nation of monarchists governed by a monarchy. As the reign advanced, the crown came increasingly to regard parliaments as merely instrumental to its own purposes. Toward the end of his life Charles found that he could survive financially, partly through the expansion of trade, which gave him a buoyant revenue, partly through a policy of peace, which recognized French ascendancy in Europe. This situation enabled him not only to breathe in comfort but to rule. "I will have no more parliaments," he was able to say, "unless it be for some necessary acts to be. passed that are temporary only, or to make new ones for the general good of the nation for God be praised my affairs are in so good a posture that I have no occasion to ask for supplies."[1]

Of England's distant, thinly settled colonies, Massachusetts had been founded on the strongest and most tenaciously held moral principles, and it was Massachusetts that had the greatest cause for immediate concern about the views of the Stuart monarch on England's throne. The reason for this was that Massachusetts also had a state religion, and there no less— perhaps even more—than in England, the maintenance of that religion was held to be the fundamental obligation of the state. Congregational ministers, who had far-reaching influence in forming opinion, never hesitated to affirm that religion was the basic justification for the existence of their state. They also had many occasions to address themselves to such other issues as the decline of religious observance and the increase of private greed; but that only served to emphasize the cardinal importance of the religious trust.

The obligations of government were certainly in every way far simpler than they have since become. In the interests of the utmost simplification they may be divided into two basic categories. The first are positive and public obligations; the second are more negative, in the sense that they are directed toward the protection of individuals. Government's positive obligations were to judge whatever questions affected the basic character of the state and to do whatever was required to maintain that character. In England's case this was defined as a monarchy linked with a national church of Protestant persuasion. Government's public obligations also naturally extended to the defense of the king's realm and to relations with foreign powers and princes. Increasingly, and unavoidably, government had to concern itself with the king's revenues and through these with the wealth of the kingdom.

Even the basic character of the state was subject to periodic redefinition according to the consequences of historical change. Under the Commonwealth it assumed that of a republic, albeit a reluctant one; after the Glorious Revolution it would come to be called a limited monarchy. Deep social and moral changes such as the rise of dissenting sects appeared as threats to the monopoly of the Church of England, just as the Protestants queried the character of the French state in a manner that Louis XIV found increasingly intolerable. When toleration became the policy of England it came not on the wings of theory but as an adaptation to facts that could not be reduced. As for the colonies, their basic character was generally less clearly defined, though it was nowhere supposed to differ in principle from that of England. Maryland and Pennsylvania, for reasons derived from their founders' beliefs, adopted a religious toleration against which the English state was still struggling until late in the century; but this did not conflict with English interests. Whenever a colony or even a substantial element in a colony defined that colony's character in ways that diverged from England's, controversy was inevitable, and conflict was always possible.

New England in general, Massachusetts in particular, were seldom entirely free from this condition. It was hardly to be expected that the matters at issue would resolve themselves simply by consulting the laws of England and making those of the colony conform to them. For one thing, although the

General Court of Massachusetts insisted as early as 1646 that the government was "framed according to our charter, and the fundamental and common law of England," a contention the court tried to demonstrate in parallel columns, the fact was that most of the laws of the colony were backed by some specific reference to the authority of the Bible—more often than not, the Old Testament.[2] But there were deeper reasons. Although social thought had not yet discovered the idea of progress and generally suspected all change as being for the worse precisely because change did threaten the character of the state, throughout the seventeenth and eighteenth centuries British society was changing. In principle, to maintain consistency between England and the colonies, it would have been necessary to ask at what point these changes had reached the stage of bringing about a change in basic character. American society, however, was also changing, and not always in the same directions.

When we set out to inquire into the obligations owed by government to the state, or to the people, we are thus embarked on a far more difficult quest than might be the case at any one definite time; for change is cumulative and carries with it changing memories. Immigrant colonists had English memories, overlaid in time with American experience; but an inevitably increasing number of colonists were not really colonists but colonials and had only American memories. Under changed conditions, colonial governments owed to their peoples different obligations from those of earlier times, and there was less and less likelihood that these would correspond to the interests of Britain. I shall suggest that the overall concept of the obligation of government underwent profound transformations in the century or so following the English Restoration and that comparable and in some respects corresponding transformations took place in the different colonies. By an ironic necessity, these comparabilities themselves clarified the differences of interest between colonial and British peoples and their governments, eventually dictating obligations which rendered them incompatible with each other. This conflict of obligations eventually convinced the colonies that they no longer belonged within the same society as their mother country.

The transformation is most dramatic in Massachusetts and is most richly documented there. Among the colonies of original settlement, Massachusetts started life with the most fully convinced sense of purpose and continued with the most articulate discussion of the problems raised by challenges to that purpose; these challenges arose from within as well as from the recurring problems of the not altogether harmonious British sense of purpose. The transformation of the concept of the obligations of government has in Massachusetts a theological, a moral, and a psychological dimension which intensifies its significance.

By contrast, the other colonies were all founded with the incentive of a very high degree of appeal to the interests of the settlers themselves. It was this rather than the service of the king or the enrichment of the state that provided the basic attraction to those colonists who at whatever level of society were able to decide to go of their own accord. It may therefore be said that the idea of private interest entered into the motivation and justification of colonial enterprise in the first half of the seventeenth century, in some cases half a century or more before it entered into the emerging language of political economy. Overall, however, these colonies were monarchies, whether directly under the crown or owned by a proprietor who owed his patent to the gift of the crown. They were all bound by the principle that they were not to depart from the laws of England although there was some doubt as to which English laws actually applied to them. Except in New England, Maryland, and Pennsylvania, they were also governed by the vague outlines of the English religious establishment, although the application was noticeably more relaxed. They were monarchies comprising the outer realms of a kingdom in which the ultimate authority—sovereignty itself—was exercised by the monarch in conjoint action with Parliament; but Parliament was nowhere mentioned in their charters. This ambiguity was to raise problems of intense feeling and exquisite intellectual difficulty.

Both in England and in New England, the first obligation of government had about it a powerful aura of divine sanction. Just as the monarchy existed by divine right and owed its obligations to God as well as to man—and was to be judged by God and not by man—so in a strong sense the New England Congregational churches owed to God the duty of maintaining the Puritan spirit and worship among the people. The second obligation was more secular. Englishmen, when possessed of a certain status mainly indicated by property or education, had certain rights pertaining to their personal security and that of their property. One of the chief reasons for the existence of government was to protect those vital attributes, notably against violation by the most potent source of danger, one or another agency of the government itself. The Restoration monarchy did not restore the courts of High Commission or Star Chamber.

These individual rights remained less prominent in Massachusetts until they were challenged, not by the old magistracy but by the regime of King James II's appointed Governor Sir Edmund Andros. The rights of Englishmen then suddenly sprang to life. According to the magistrates and divines of Massachusetts, the purpose of their society was to live in the fellowship of Christ as understood by the Puritans, "where all, or the most considerable part of the free Planters profess their desire and purpose of enjoying and securing to themselves and their Posterity, the pure and peaceful enjoyment of the Ordinances of Christ in Church-fellowship with his People, and have liberty to cast themselves into that Mould or Form of a Commonwealth, which shall appear best for them."[3] These were the words of John Davenport, writing about "a New Plantation whose Design is Religion," in reply to a writer who had had the temerity to hold that civil government ought to be taken out of the hands of the church. Davenport stood wholly within the traditions of Massachusetts when he insisted that where the object of society was religion, it could be served only by limiting both political rights and magistracy to church members.

It was conventional for the ministry to link the state with its religious design and aim. No Puritan minister was more eloquent than William Hubbard in explaining the connection between the social order and the providential design of the universe. The happiness of a people, he explained in 1676 in a sermon significantly given that rather secular title, was to be found in a state of order: "Such a disposition of things, themselves equall and unequal, as gives to every one their due and proper place. Beauty arises from symmetry; the heavens were disposed in ranks and orders of cherubims, seraphims, archangels and angels."[4] This cosmic image was a conventional example of the place of man in the Great Chain of Being and the corresponding organization of civil government in man's society. A comparable harmony should prevail between rulers and ruled; the rulers had a duty to listen, the ruled should obey. Hubbard's case for respecting rank was based on a direct appeal to the intentions of the Almighty, who had created earthly ranks as much from his regard for human nature as from his own wisdom and power. Without the leadership of those of superior rank, the foolish and ignorant would lose themselves in the wilderness. "The fearful and weak might be destroyed, if others more strong and valient, did not defend them."[5] He must have had his eye on someone who had been suggesting that rank was not part of the order of nature when he declared—picking up an echo from Ecclesiastes but blocking its earthly meaning—that "nothing therefore can be imagined more remote either from

7

right reason, or true religion, than to think that because we all once were equal at our birth, and shall be again at our death, that therefore we should be so in the whole course of our lives." Yet Hubbard recognized that religion was voluntary; religion "without the will's consent is nothing."[6] And there is a strong hint of the need for toleration on the part of civil rulers. Toleration in religion: but he then mounted an attack on the two faults, which were the cause of God's quarrel with the province. The first was spiritual pride, which sprang up with genuine good works, but which led to disorder and contention; the other was worldly-mindedness and covetousness.[7] Although Increase Mather, at this time emerging as a claimant to be the chief spokesman of the more orthodox Puritan persuasion, next year replied to Hubbard's tolerationist arguments, both these men were inspired by a consistent sense of the hierarchy of the universe according to God's intent. It was therefore wholly in keeping that Mather was soon afterward arguing, with considerable biblical authority, that the children of godly parents had the advantage in the prospects of salvation.[8] The two ministers may have had rival political aims, but they both sensed that men arranged themselves according to God's patterns that they might dance to his music.

From a later standpoint it became easy to see that this world of harmony based on natural order of which human society was a part would one day break up. Perhaps it was already beginning. As early as 1652 the General Court had ordained a fast to atone, in addition to the usual sins, for "the worldly mindedness, oppression, & hardhartedness feared to be among us."[9] The synod of 1679 denounced ten sins, of which the tenth was "Inordinate affection unto the world."[10] Advancing material interests, the disorderly complexity of political rivalries, war, trade, and geographical expansion would one day bring a different world into existence, and ministers were already keenly aware of the threat. Urian Oakes, pleading with

New Englanders to keep religious precepts in their economic lives, denounced "Griping and Squeezing, and grinding the Faces of the Poor, and Greediness there is among us . . . Hence a private, Selfish spirit." Nor had the Lord given them permission to be levelers and libertines, "to do every man what seems good to his own eyes. Thus far he hath delivered us from Anarchy and Confusion, as well as from Tyranny." But material aims were taking possession. "There is so much rooting in the EARTH, there is little growing upward, Heavenward, I mean: Men are coupling both Worlds together (as one speaks) that they may drive them both before them." [11] Increase Mather warned his congregation that the abounding of iniquity told of trouble at hand. [12] It was; two years later the country was ravaged by King Philip's war. Mather then came more directly to the issue of economic motivation: "since *Day-Labourers* and *Mechanicks* are so unreasonable in their demands, and *Merchants* (some of them) so excessive in the prizes they set upon their goods, it is enough to bring the *Oppressing Sword*." [13]

The people of Massachusetts were well aware that they had different interests to promote than the people of England; and in addition, sharp differences had developed among themselves. But in face of domestic opposition their leaders maintained a self-regarding view of their English property and political rights. To protect those rights was as much an obligation of government but only, it seemed, so far as they were consistent with its religious character. Those merchants who did not subscribe to the Congregational religion were in a sense more English than the dominant rulership. The Andros regime had the effect of throwing them together. Within this framework the Massachusetts revolt against Andros stands out as a fairly simple event. Its background contains nothing like the complex interweaving of ideology, religion, and conflicts of interest that grew up in the eighteenth century, and its interpretation does not involve the subtleties of the American Revolution. Andros violated the religious susceptibilities of the majority of New Englanders, taxed them without their consent, and called in their land titles; members of his council were reported to have openly told protesters that they were slaves, "the only difference between them and slaves is their not being bought and sold."[14] All this was not the result of possibly ill-informed or misguided regulation by a distant government that could be reasoned with on its own principles. It sprang from opposing principles, striking at the essence of New England's foundation, and was a direct, physical invasion of New England's liberties and religion.

Yet this regime was also, unfortunately, an indication that the colonies were governed by the crown. In England James II employed executive proclamations and other instruments of royal power and was able to pass his demands through compliant courts of justice. Parliament had no agency in the colonies, and in truth there was little ground for believing that it would have much to do with the future government even of England itself. But the history, social structure, and religious dispositions of England were infinitely more complex than those of the province, and the problem of getting rid of James raised difficulties to the full measure of those complexities; it could not have been solved without foreign intervention. By contrast, the revolt against Andros, although not without its own complexities of timing and motive, was a comparatively straightforward action with the very simple objective of restoring the original character of the state. The only way to do this was to resume the charter given by Charles I in 1629.

Yet this faith was based on an illusion. A resumption of the old charter was impossible because the crown had every reason to be dissatisfied with the conduct of Massachusetts under that charter. Even if resumption had been politically possible, however, the old leaders could not have reversed the change that was creeping over the province, a change so profound that it must one day bring about a transformation in the basic character of the state, which has usually been described as a process of secularization.[15] No reader of the records would be likely to challenge this identification. It might, however, be timely to rename it, or at least to recognize that secularization was itself a product of a broader transmutation, which can better be called diversification.[16] The clergy could not keep a grip on all the interests of a rapidly multiplying diversity of individuals, not all of which could perhaps be easily dignified as callings. The principal long-term effect was to assimilate the New England provinces more closely to those further south—and west, in the case of New York. A promotional broadside as early as 1665 appealing for settlers in the Duke of York's territories actually challenged the Boston authorities on their own ground by offering liberty of conscience in the Protestant religion together with freedom to choose town officers; and this was printed in Boston, with the obvious intention of attracting migrants dissatisfied with religious intolerance.[17] Later, and on a still broader base, when William Penn wanted to encourage settlement in his territories, he gave Magna Carta its first printing on American soil and subtitled his pamphlet "Being the Birth-right of the Free-born subjects of England."[18] The rulers of Massachusetts had not in the past seen fit to extend their concept of English rights to religious dissent and had proved notably touchy about political dissidence. Even after the Restoration, they had hanged Quakers who refused to quit Boston under warning, and they had no soft sentiments about liberty of the press. As Thomas Hutchinson, living in the changed atmosphere of the Enlightenment, later sardonically remarked, under Andros's censorship the press merely changed its keeper.[19] Witches or women, presumably did not qualify for the rights of Englishmen, so the periodic witch executions took only their lives, not their rights.

The clergy certainly did not abandon their mission. That

would be a complete misconception. But in the years that followed the Glorious Revolution it became difficult to keep up the claim that the governments of the New England provinces were concerned above all with the religious order. Not only was the struggle itself political, but some of the leading clergy became politicians; Increase Mather took charge as the province's principal negotiator with the English government. The success of the revolt entailed political consequences, which were made much more acute by the unwelcome discovery that the new English authorities fully intended to maintain their predecessors' interest in the internal affairs of New England. The implications of this interest, and the gradually emerging role of Parliament, took some time to absorb and still longer to interpret. They were neither quickly nor clearly understood.

It was only under the Andros regime that New Englanders, and especially their acknowledged leaders, began to discover how English they really were. In the dense outcropping of pamphlets surrounding the Andros affair, New England spokesmen began to identify themselves not only as bearing English rights but as having interests in common with the English people, as they had never had occasion to do before.[20] No one made this argument more persuasively than Increase Mather, writing in reply to a tract by the Andros attorney general, John Palmer. He began by calling New England's enemies "Tory adversaries" and added New England's claim to be not only Protestant but Church of England. He admitted but played down some points in which the first planters "did not indeed comply with several things imposed in the Church of England which they thought unwarrantable." Compliance would have been sinful. After answering Palmer's thesis that the colonies were conquered provinces like Wales and Ireland, Mather asserted that only a common enemy could thus deny English liberties. "No Englishmen in their wits," he said, "will venture their lives and estates to enlarge the King's dominions and enrich the whole English nation, to be rewarded by being deprived of English liberties."[21]

This point deserves attention because it not only makes the very tendentious claim that the planters ventured forth with the object of enriching England, but it was probably the first prominent public assertion that the interests of England were involved with the fortunes of New England. He made it very explicit a moment later: "And pray, let all the English *American* plantations now take notice, that the *New Englanders* in their late Revolution did but act in a *quarrel* in which *they* and, *all* Englishmen had an interest." Mather was visibly on the defensive against criticism from other colonies; but he pressed a very nice legal argument to the effect that New England was actually considered part of England on the ground that the Quo Warranto writs against New England had named them as belonging to the English manors of Westminster and Greenwich.[22] Such an identification may have helped with the case for English rights; but it raised serious problems of colonial legislative power, and in longer perspective one can see that it might have allowed the possibility of a greater degree of English authority than Massachusetts could comfortably live with. The English identity had been asserted in political terms by Hubbard of Ipswich in a manuscript history written in 1688, which claimed that the form of government of the early foundation was "attempered with the greatest resemblance to that of our own kingdom of England, and the several corporations thereof." The people, he explained in a rather obscure passage, were involved in the process by which taxes were laid, and there was no arbitrary power or unusual administration of justice.[23] It is clear that both theologically and politically, the England to which Mather and Hubbard referred was the England of their dreams, uncorrupted by Laud or Charles I.

John Palmer's attack on the rebels, however, caused consternation. If not in all respects very convincing, it needed answering because he lanced the former regime at some vulnerable points. Apart from the dangerous theory that assimilated the American colonies to Wales and Ireland, he argued with unpleasant plausibility that the Andros administration had caused offense to leading New Englanders over the Navigation Acts precisely because it had enforced them. In the matter of religion, Palmer acidly observed that the Dominion gave freedom of conscience after many of "The King's subjects had groaned under the severity of a Tyrannical and Arbitrary Constitution deprived of the Laws and Liberties of Englishmen," and some "suffered death for Religion." As for higher motives, Palmer accused his enemies of acting out of self-interest, fondness for "their former popular Government, and aversion to the Government established from *England*." The pamphlet significantly took the form of a letter addressed to the clergy and ended with a request to that body to admonish the people.[24]

Within a few months Edward Rawson had joined Increase Mather in defense and counterattack. Rawson was particularly concerned to refute Palmer's insinuation that New Englanders were "Commonwealthsmen, Enemies to Monarchy and to the Church of England," though all he could find to say by way of refutation was "that's such a sham as everyone sees through." Like Mather, Rawson insisted on the identification of New England's revolt with the Glorious Revolution—as it was one day to be called. "No man," he said, "does really approve of the *Revolution* in *England*, but must justifie that in *New England* also."[25]

In refuting Palmer's argument that the colonies resembled Wales and Ireland, Rawson fell back on a distinction which would not have boded well for the future of colonial unity. His defense applied, it seems, specifically to the New England plantations; but in Barbados, Jamaica, and Virginia the assemblies owed their existence only to "the favour of the prince."[26] This statement implies that when assemblies were called into being by grace of the royal prerogative, that call did not establish any corresponding right to popular self-government. It was the duty of rulers to protect the rights of individuals; against tyranny people had always the right of rebellion. Government was always and everywhere under an obligation to protect the people; but these views in turn implied that the people had some claim to hold the government to its obligation, and recent events had given this question of accountability an extraordinary prominence. But even so, the right to rebel was an extreme remedy to an extreme crisis. It had nothing whatever to do with day-to-day government or the administration of justice. No specific theory of representation could have been inferred from Rawson's pages, and his views were a long way from any conception of democracy.

Two themes begin to emerge from this discussion. The first, from the Massachusetts point of view, is external, or at least is imposed on Massachusetts by virtue of the English connection. The leadership, realistically adapting itself to the exigencies of English politics, identified the interests of the province with those of England to an unprecedented degree. Increase Mather was in no doubt that this policy was the essential foundation for the measure of independence which the old leadership hoped to preserve under the new monarchy. But it was never entirely popular. It was subjected to a persistent, resentful, and irreconcilable opposition by a group led by Elisha Cooke, which merged into the so-called "Country" party to survive as a permanent feature of Massachusetts politics. Under frequently changing political conditions and intermittent impulses of imperial control from the British authorities, the accommodationist policy encountered vicissitudes and opportunities, which also varied under different royal governors. In the last analysis, the acceptance of royal authority marked the recognition of necessity by the official leadership. The opposition's policy could well have driven the crown to the one step that Massachusetts successfully averted down to the Revolution—withdrawal of the charter. Accommodation in any case became increasingly easy to reconcile to the defense needs of the province during the long wars with France. But the opposition was more, as a rule, than a conventional parliamentary opposition to the "court" as represented by governor, council, and assembly majority; it was tinged with undying resentment against the Charter of 1691. And in country areas it was not free of expressions of disloyalty to the crown itself.[27]

The second theme pertains to the internal subject matter of politics, itself in the long run no less fundamental to the question of the character of the state. Setting aside the questions that sprang up around the personality of Governor Joseph Dudley, the issues that dominated internal politics were increasingly connected with economic interests rather than with religious hegemony. And when both political pamphleteers and Congregational ministers spoke of "interests," as they increasingly did, they meant those of merchants, fishermen, shipwrights, builders (or carpenters), domestic craftsmen, and of course the various grades of farmers. The use of this language in turn gradually introduced into political thinking the idea that the pursuit of interest was the legitimate concern of economic life and therefore of political life whenever the interests sought political protection or advantage. This trend was admitted with manifest discomfort and reluctance in New England but was in keeping with the thinking of the times. William Penn had observed that "interest has the security though not the virtue of a principle." The crux of the matter was to recognize the legitimacy of interest and by that means to convert it into the strongest incentive to good behavior. The problem was coming to be seen in that light by English philosophers before the end of the 1680s.[28]

Since the clergy was entrusted with responsibility for the safety of religion and was coming to be the only group who could be counted on to regard it as a primary object of the state's existence, it is instructive to follow through the annual election sermons the increasing concentration on the secular qualities of rulers which resulted from the diversification of the activities of the people. The tension between the old and new views of the state was clearly expressed and as clearly resolved in an important sermon by the conservative minister Samuel Willard in 1694. Both its title—*The Character of a Good Ruler*—and argument give it, even at this early date, a certain salience in marking the shifting distribution of weights in the balance of political thought. One striking statement, that "A People are not made for Rulers, but Rulers for a People," can too easily be extracted and given an artificial prominence as an indication of the progress of popular ideas. But it would be misleading to read this remark as a clue to Willard's tone and meaning. His emphasis is on rulers; that is why he must insist that they exist for the people. All the same, there is a difference between putting the emphasis this way rather than on the service of God. Many practical benefits flowed from good government, and there was much to be said for having a good charter; but it was the good ruler who made the people happy even under a good charter. There is very little sign here of government by consent; it comes in as a bonus, hardly as a right.

Both the original inspiration of government and its guiding principles are of divine ordination. But the multiplication of mankind would have made government necessary even if the Fall had never happened. The principles that govern men therefore fall squarely into the natural frame, with all the superiority and subordination that are essential to the natural order of the universe; this principle had not changed since Hubbard's sermon of 1676, long before the rebellion, and perhaps that event had made it imperative to warn the people that subordination to rulers was indeed the order of the universe and not a mere trick passed off by rulers onto their subjects. We may take Willard's argument a little further for him by observing that when Andros imposed a rule that conflicted with God's design it was Andros who fell; nothing had happened to upset the ruling principle. The word of God, Willard continued, recommends the character of a good ruler; the people have very little to do but to obey and get on with their business. It is well worth taking note of the place of this thinking in the context of the profound disturbance to long-received truths that had been initiated in Europe by the questionings of Descartes, by Newton's investigations of the laws of the natural order, through the philosophy, psychology, and politics of Leibnitz and Locke, to name only the most widely read at the time.[29] There is not a breath of all this intellectual questioning in Willard, nor of the concept of *virtù*, which was to enter prominently into the thought of the Enlightenment from sources in Italian humanism.[30] Willard speaks a language which would have been as foreign to Thomas Jefferson and his associates as the language of George III's ministers—in one important respect more so, for they had no room for divine inspiration as a justification of government and rested their claims for political authority on more pragmatic grounds.

Back in the early 1670s prominent ministers had occasion to worry about the forms of extortion practiced by artisans and merchants who possessed rare skills or precious commodities.[31] If this theme was not so sustained in the 1680s it is most likely to have been because the crown's quarrel with New England distracted attention from God's; soon after the Glorious Revolution, the clergy returned to a persistent anxiety about the pursuit of private interest, particularly when this was done at the expense of the public. There were other dangers to worry about, for in 1690 Cotton Mather warned the people that "relics of our former oppressors have sown among us dissensions."[32] Perhaps Anglicans were unhappy about the reimposition of the rule of the former saints; Mather did not explain. When clergymen got involved in political issues, they may have been moved by the need to defend the religious character of the state; but the commitment entailed the support of specific economic policies, which could only lead them into an irretrievably secular strain. Thus Cotton Mather himself was soon to be heard supporting the expedition against Quebec, which no doubt had an anti-Roman and therefore religious motive; but as a necessary consequence, Mather supported also the province's paper money, which would be kept there "where it will (or at least) ought" to be accepted as legal tender.[33] By 1695 he was openly alarmed by the threat posed to the order and values of the community by those who flaunted the self-justifying ethics of getting rich quick. "A righteous man misses many an advantage that is taken by those that *make haste to be Rich*. But then, the *Little Money* which he gets has no *Rust* upon it."[34] This sermon conveys a compassion for those who fail in the struggle that was to lose most of its force with the rising thrust of what we now call economic individualism: "Losers may still be beloved of God,"[35] Cotton reminded the winners in his congregation. It was obvious that he was talking to men who fully intended to go on making money, so the best thing to do was to tell them to use it with moderation. He warned the ambitious merchants of Boston that they were merely stewards of their property and should prepare to make an account of their stewardship to God. Men were allowed to lay up something for their children but should consecrate the rest "to more pious uses."[36] These material concerns made it increasingly necessary to stress that rulers should be men of "knowledge and ability" as well as being "faithful."[37]

Clerical eloquence unfortunately did not entirely dissipate the temptations of self-advancement, which tended increasingly to set up a dangerous schism between private wealth and public interest. The elder Mather found himself compelled, in a lament on King William's death in 1702, to develop much more fully the theme he had opened up nearly thirty years earlier.[38] At that time it was specified classes who took advantage of special shortages, a condition that might be regarded as temporary; but now the pursuit of gain seems to have become more widespread and reckless. Taking as his epigraph the words, "Seeking the wealth of the People"— that is, not of the individual—Increase taught the doctrine "That Rulers ought to be of a Publick Spirit, Seeking the Welfare of their People, so when they are such, it will be their lasting Renown." The rulers undoubtedly held the burden of responsibility for the state: the "welfare or ilfare" of the people depended very much on their rulers and also on the laws and on the protection of liberty and property. "Next to Religion," he said, carrying the emphasis forward to secular and libertarian considerations, "the happiness of a People consists in Civil Liberties." This was assuredly an advance on the spiritual leadership afforded under the first charter. But even so, not all were guided by these precepts, and Mather warned against "particular interests," which had led individuals to transgress the law made for the public good by the General Assembly and had thereby hurt the whole country. "The evil of a self-seeking spirit" had many harmful effects, but Mather was too experienced and too good a Christian to try to separate evil men from unpolluted ones. "It is sadly true," he admitted, "that there is too much of evil in good men." Christianity now came back to block the appeal to self-interest. "A man cannot be a disciple of Christ except he deny himself" (Matthew 16:24). And he concluded this section of his argument by offering as an appropriate epitaph for a self-seeker: "Here lies a man that sought himself while he lived, and lost himself when he dyed."[39]

Both the political literature and the sermons of subsequent years increasingly reflected a burning quest for guidance in the problems of economic and monetary policy that occupied men's minds.[40] If theology lost its pride of place in the obligations of government, it would hardly be true or fair to say that government ceased to be concerned with maintaining a moral order. In this respect the role of government was larger and more complex than ever before. For government alone could attempt to reconcile the complex tensions involved in maintaining a larger view of the purposes of the state while catering to the legitimate pursuit of private aims. In a sense it became the more difficult obligation of government to keep in being a general view of the character and interest of the people as a whole while serving that of some of its more fortunate or energetic members. No moral or theological power could check the advance of the politics of interest. "Private interest is the string in the bear's nose," Henry Care had said, in an English work which enjoyed long-lived popularity in the colonies.[41] "Interest bears great sway with men," Anthony Stoddard confessed in a Connecticut election sermon in 1716; "that what men can't be persuaded to, by any means, when they conceive their Interest may be served thereby, they will apply themselves to it whatsoever it may be." The emphasis in this as in so many election sermons was on the powers of rulers and the duty of the ruled to obey. The opening of Romans 13, "The powers that be are ordained of God"—probably the most popular election sermon epigraph—was here in evidence. The people must obey their rulers, apply themselves to their own business, and desire the prosperity of all. Americans were already revealing a certain characteristic impatience for quick satisfactions, which Hutchinson later commented on when writing about the land bank of 1740. Travelers from Europe, he said, often observed this colonial unwillingness to sacrifice a present convenience or delight even though it must cause future distress. By 1730 Thomas Foxcroft was sufficiently complacent about New England's prosperity to maintain that it actually stemmed from the religious spirit of the people; both prosperity and the growth of population were compared favorably with those of the plantation that had been made for gain.[42] This flattering image could have held very little comfort for the people of Massachusetts as their conditions got steadily worse while those of New York and Pennsylvania improved.

By flagrant disregard for the Navigation Acts, by repeated quarrels with royal governors, and particularly by refusals to vote a permanent salary, Massachusetts made itself a candidate for hostile scrutiny in Whitehall and even in Westminster. Jeremiah Dummer was becoming alarmed by new threats to the independence of the province when he sat down to compose his well-known *Defence of the New England Charters* in 1721.[43] He was already uneasy at this seemingly early date by rumors reaching England that Massachusetts entertained vague yearnings for independence. "It is a generally receiv'd Opinion," he both admitted and warned, "that the People in the Plantations have an Interest distinct from that of the Crown—" from which it was held to follow that too much power could not be given to governors or too little to the people. The reverse, he claimed, was the truth. The thrust of Dummer's argument was that Great Britain derived great benefit from the plantations, that this benefit arose from commerce, and that commerce flourished in conditions of liberty. In reply to the British fear that the charter colonies would grow great and formidable, and to the British suspicions that increasing numbers and wealth would lead to a desire for independence, Dummer advanced the argument that it was the rise of the colonies that enabled them to contribute so materially to Britain's wealth. "It were no difficult Task," he declared, in what was surely one of the most resounding blows of the prolonged argument about the benefits of empire in the eighteenth century, "to prove that London has risen out of the Plantations, and not out of England."[44]

Dummer was too well-informed to deny the supremacy of the legislative power, by which he meant the power to make or amend the laws that determined the fundamental character of the state. The question, however, "is not about Power, but about Right. *And shall not the Supream Judicature of all the*

Nation do right? One may say, that what the parliament can't do justly, they can't do at all."[45] The quotation is adapted from Genesis; and it is not without interest that one observes the legislature being transposed into the place of the Deity.[46] These are very interesting remarks. They begin to anticipate the rather involved arguments by which, some thirty years later, James Otis acknowledged parliamentary power while denying that Parliament could effectively contravene the common law.[47] Dummer was at pains to deny the slightest suggestion of a colonial drift toward independence, although he was not beyond using the opinion that such a drift existed as an indirect warning to Britain. One of his main achievements was to place the justification for the existing constitutional arrangements, so difficult to define in legal terms, squarely on the pragmatic grounds of their manifest success. Prosperity was proving the question of right. This shift from an implicit (if grumbling) acceptance of royal authority to a pragmatic basis of justification became increasingly characteristic of colonial argumentation. Since the argument directed all attention toward the advantages of the imperial connection, it was easy to overlook the deeper significance of the underlying assumption, which was that the colonies were in fact separate political entities which could decide whether or not the connection with Britain was to their advantage. The adoption of this theme was to have as yet barely suspected implications when Parliament did use its powers to control not merely the trade but the internal affairs of the colonies.

While the colonies to the southward increased in prosperity and in the diversity of their operations, Massachusetts was afflicted with growing difficulties. The available money was not enough for the circulation of goods, exports even including the rum that was produced from West Indian molasses failed to balance the terms of overseas trade, and the agriculture of the province was unable to produce enough food to supply the people, especially those of Boston, whose periodic shortages aggravated the distress of a growing body of the chronically poor.[48] Exhortations to piety would not have made much impression on these problems.

In the midst of all this, and not without connections with the general conditions of economic and social stress, the Great Awakening split many communities asunder and raised the most disturbing challenge to constituted authority in the churches themselves. In the light of all that we have so far seen of ministers accommodating themselves to the realities of economic pressures and political power, it does not come as any great surprise to find that some of their congregations began to feel a real sense of spiritual deprivation. According to reports reaching Boston, where *The American Magazine* of intercolonial interest had recently been launched—it was not to last for long—complaints that "practical" sermons failed to satisfy spiritual needs had been heard before the Awakening began.[49] I have no desire to add to the already large literature of social, economic, and psychological, not to say religious interpretation of the Great Awakening; but I do suggest one significant negative point, if only because it does not appear to have been made before. For all its dynamic effects on peoples' lives and its often shattering impact on local churches and communities, the Awakening did not renew the old sense of the religious responsibility of government or lead to demands that the clergy should once again become linked with the legislators in giving laws to the people. The assembly was obliged to concern itself with Baptist demands for equal religious rights, to which it accommodated within limits and without good grace. But at no time did it have to respond to, nor did the Awakening make any demand to restore, the theological character of the state. All the agencies of government, whether royal, judicial, or representative, looked on their duties to the crown, the law, and the people in a light that had become purely secular, entirely occupied with considerations of war, trade, land, poverty, and population.[50]

When some of the excitement had begun to subside, the Reverend Ebenezer Gay, on being invited to deliver the annual election sermon, chose a theme and title reminiscent of the past but symbolic of the transformations of half a century. Taking his key from Samuel Willard, he called it *The Character and Work of a Good Ruler, and the Duty of an Obliged People*. So "work" is added to amplify the qualifications of "character," and the people too have explicit duties, an obligation owed in return for good rulership. Here at last was an indication of the popular presence in government.

The relationship between rulers and ruled was, as usual, reciprocal but unequal. The idea that would have corresponded to the existence of democratic government, that of a continuous political accountability on the part of rulers to the ruled, nowhere appears in these colonial election sermons. For Gay as for his colleagues over a lengthy period, it was the rulers who made the rules; he was to enlighten the people with a knowledge of peace, directing them in the way of duty and safety; he was a comfort to his people; under him peace and good order were preserved: "Innumerable are the Benefits which People receive from good Government." A good ruler would seek the wealth of his people and would speak peace to them. But he would encounter difficulties from perverse spirits, from murmuring and fightings against him, and from envy which sought to undermine him. The people ought to be concerned for the preservation of a good ruler.

The spirit of benevolence, which was playing an increasingly prominent part in the political thought reaching the colonies from England and Scotland, was consonant with the qualities required by the good ruler. It would be an error to regard this as a concession to advancing materialism. Benevolence was a way of attributing to God somewhat more benign and gentle qualities than had prevailed among the Puritans or seemed sometimes to be held by the revivalists. A recurring theme in Gay's sermon was that the ruler's character resembled that of light; and this image may have been adopted as a reply to the revivalist claim that they, the awakened, were the ones who had seen the "new light." The good ruler stood forth as an example of "charity and greatness of understanding, and Depth of Penetration, pureness of Design, Benignity of Temper, Warmth of Public Spirit, Constancy and Activity in Provident Care, Steadiness of Proceeding, and the most diffusive Benevolence."[51] If these remarks were directed to the governor, William Shirley, rather than to the elected representatives, he told the latter (when electing the council) to choose men who would forego their own ease and private advantage for the public weal. This benign if by that time rather bland catalog of virtues derives its significance from the contemporary thinking it reflected. Assumptions about the basic structure of authority had changed very little but had at least begun to let the people into the picture, even if only by way of reminding them of their duties; the land bank episode had no doubt served to suggest that many of them were in need of the reminder, so the concession was more significant than it was made to appear. Benevolence had entered into the character of the deity, which in turn meant that people had begun to enjoy a right to be happy. And finally, the qualities listed were entirely secular. There was not a word here of obligation to maintain a social order operating under divine dispensation and seeking divine inspiration for the sake of a godly commonwealth; even the divine right of rulers had thinned into a general authority which seems not unconnected with their ability to maintain the prescribed standards.

These tones may still have been somewhat less familiar in New England than elsewhere, but they were in keeping with their times. "Cato," the pseudonymous author of the essays of the British independent Whig writers John Trenchard and Thomas Gordon, had observed that no government now on earth owed its beginning to the immediate revelation of God or could derive its existence from such revelation. The only causes of government were human ones.[52] And the Scottish philosopher Francis Hutcheson observed that no form of government could be esteemed more divine than any other; the only test was its ability to promote the prosperity of the community.[53] It could only follow that mankind was at liberty to choose his own form of polity. The transformation, as I have suggested, is most dramatic in Massachusetts because Massachusetts had a political order originally derived from a religious purpose. In 1744 a contributor to the Boston press asserted that the true object of loyalty was "a good legal constitution" rather than the authority and interest of one man— an argument which sets the constitution above the monarch.[54] In other colonies the process of diversification had from the beginning been a diversification of secular aims. But these secular aims were themselves being subtly transmuted into justifications for government itself. Mines were being laid, which could one day blow up the foundations even of royal authority.

John Peter Zenger, whose newspaper, *The New-York Weekly Journal*, had been founded to speak for the Morrisite faction in the contentious politics of New York, was the instrument through which these themes were brought into the political dialogue of the province. He achieved a large measure of this by simply reprinting the essays of Cato. Much of Zenger's material must be read in the light of the Morrisites' running battle with Governor William Cosby and the assembly over liberty of the press as against previous censorship (which incidentally had not existed in Britain since the lapse of the Licensing Act of 1695). But that does nothing to diminish the force of the argument. And Cato had no great faith in the automatic benevolence of government, writing: "Power without control appertains to God alone; and no Man ought to be trusted with what no Man is equal to."[55] A little earlier Cato had been quoted to the effect that security of property was always associated with freedom of speech—which, significantly, was why Charles I had tried to suppress free speech. The connection hinted at between any modern administration which tried to interfere with free speech and the reign of Charles I was not likely to be missed; and what lay in store, one might ask, for governments that tampered with liberty and property? Cato went on to assert, "The Administration of Government, is nothing less than the attendance of the trustees of the People upon the Interest, and Affairs of the People."[56]

It is profoundly significant of the colonial style of thought, a style which very gradually took the form of an American ideology, that it carried with it so little resonance of the old, deep-seated English royalist sentiment. Monarchy might be a fact, and the better a man's education the more likely he was to approve of it as a political necessity. But these opinions failed to evoke much corresponding emotion. There were "court" interests in all the colonies, in one sense or another; by the time of agonizing decision from 1774 to 1776, many Americans emerged—many more no doubt concealed themselves—as Loyalists. As such they were called "Tories" by their enemies, who preferred to style themselves "Whigs" after the opposition to James II. But in the true British sense, there were few genuine American Tories, for it was easier for an American to become a "tory" in the special American sense of the word, resulting directly from the split over independence, than to identify himself with the historic loyalties that connected the British Tory with church and throne.[57] English society continued to contain a large proportion of genuine Tories who never felt fully represented by the parliaments that Sir Robert Walpole so effectively controlled and through which he built up the great Whig oligarchy, which gathered to itself the mantle of loyalty to the Hanoverian throne.

English Tory thought contained at least a substratum of the doctrine of passive obedience. One is tempted to say that by contrast this doctrine was totally absent from colonial thought; that, certainly, would be the inference from colonial sermons and other writings. But it would not be entirely correct. In 1750 the Reverend Jonathan Mayhew achieved more than local prominence by delivering a blast at this very doctrine of "Unlimited Submission and Non-Resistance" that was so notable by its absence. The date of his sermon heralded the approach of 30 January—the execution of Charles the Martyr—on which date "the *slavish* doctrine of passive obedience and nonresistance is often warmly asserted." So we learn that Anglican priests were in the habit of reminding their congregations of the fate and example of Charles I on that day; but it is surely of equal significance that we learn this from Mayhew, because not one such sermon was ever printed.[58] It would also be prudent to be cautious about the inferences to be drawn from Mayhew's rhetoric. In the first place, we have no record of what the Anglicans actually said; in the second, their sermons are not at all likely to have advocated passive obedience as a positive precept, if only because it was not a live issue in immediate politics, and to mention it could have done no obvious good. (It might even have been taken as an injunction to obey the Congregationalist authorities of New England.) Both Mayhew's strictures and the Anglican sermons he attacked are best read in the context of the renewal of the struggle for a Church of England bishopric in the colonies—and not merely in the colonies but in Boston itself. In that light the faintest whisper of the doctrine becomes more ominous, because the powers that would come to be in the future would of course be those of the archbishop of Canterbury and the king himself.[59]

It is difficult to find other traces. Benjamin Prescott, in a pamphlet appealing for calm and restraint written in 1768 but published six years later, alludes to "Times, when the doctrine of passive Obedience was preach'd up to the Heighth," but trusted that those times would not return.[60]

Mayhew did much more than stuff Whig words down the trumpets of the Church of England—in language for which he was correctly accused by his enemies of plagiarism; he achieved the remarkable feat of converting Romans 13 into a Whig tract, a performance which would have astonished the Apostle but mightily pleased many of the Congregationalists of Massachusetts. Mayhew found it "obvious . . . that the rulers whom the Apostle here speaks of, and obedience to whom he presses upon Christians as a duty, are *good rulers*, such as are, in the exercise of their office and power, benefactors to society."[61] This was an advance on the good-natured precepts of Ebenezer Gay, by whom the young Mayhew had been influenced, for now the people owed obedience to their rulers only to the extent that they proved themselves to be *good* rulers. For this turn of the argument, Mayhew gave a justification frankly founded on utility: "The true ground and reason of our obligation to be subject to the higher powers is the usefulness of magistracy (when properly exercised) to human society and its subserviency to the general welfare."[62]

Mayhew's forceful language stirred up an immediate controversy. Anglicans lashed back and reopened the debate about the virtues of Charles I and the lawfulness of his government. Nor was Mayhew's rationalist Arminianism acceptable to all of his colleagues; but his chief opposition came from those who regarded his views as heretical for religious, not for political reasons. The absence, or feebleness, of a genuinely royalist opposition to the political implications of these views represents one of the negative forces in colonial thought. This silence, this absence of ancient continuities with European institutions, helps to give the appearance of positive presence to "Whig" thought, or even to the old "Commonwealth" traditions.

There is no need to attribute a seriously republican leaning to this style of thought. Yet Americans were distinctly lacking in old Stuart loyalties or royalist sentiments. William Livingston, writing in his own *Independent Reflector*, felt perfectly free to say in 1753 that he approved of the execution of Charles I, who was "too weak for a King, too powerful for a Subject."[63] Such an expression would have been risky in Britain, where royal executions were not considered a favorable precedent. It was not at all common, for that matter, in America, but at least such sentiments could be published there without risk of social ostracism or, worse, suspicions of treasonous intent.

Livingston, who later in life became a longtime governor of New Jersey, was not writing election sermons but was no less concerned with the relation between rulers and ruled. Like most educated Americans of his day, he strongly approved of the English constitutional compound of monarchy, aristocracy, and democracy, "infinitely the best." Livingston insistently emphasized the necessity of government, but he recognized that the object of government was to produce conditions for popular happiness. "The true Happiness of a People consists in the Wisdom of their Governors," he explained—but the ruler's "Passions and Interest" should "center in the Happiness of his People."[64] Livingston's strong defense of liberty and property, which he associated with the rule of law and with the supposedly voluntary and egalitarian basis on which society was originally formed, was reinforced by quotations from Locke's *Second Treatise*; and in a linking action which had become a commonplace of English constitutional thought but was nevertheless subject to widely differing shades of meaning, depending on who made the assertion and about what government, he upheld the Glorious Revolution as authority for resistance in defense of liberties.[65]

When political partisans took up particular issues they made a common assumption. If it lay in the power of the provincial government to correct abuses or to protect or assist some group of merchants, manufacturers, or fishermen, or for that matter even some religious sect, then government—from the General Court downward—had a duty to do so. The secular nature of such concerns could be taken for granted in all but the religious cases, and about them there was more doubt as to where the duty of government lay. But colonial writings were beginning to register a newer assumption, making its way into the colonies from the writings of British philosophers and even from the arminianizing influences of the English church. This was nothing less than the duty of government to promote the happiness of the people. Writers such as Livingston said so again and again. But their predecessors of earlier generations had not said so. Government—usually meaning the peoples' own elected representatives—was engaged with problems of livelihoods and standards of living. All of its operations in these ordinary connections were dwarfed by its operation in time of war; and the 1740s saw the opening of a new period of spasmodic but prolonged military and naval warfare which touched American coasts, reached along inland waters, and lacerated the frontiers. In peace, and in many aspects of life that were not militarily connected, it was still true that government weighed lightly on the shoulders of colonists when compared with the burdens of the peoples of Europe. But government clearly had to discharge the duty of its old protective role and secure the individual in his personal status. In all these ways it is no exaggeration to say that by mid-century something of a consensus was emerging that government owed to the people the obligation of creating and defending the conditions of their happiness. Not their happiness itself: given freedom, that was their own affair.

What, in these changing circumstances, did people owe to government? Men in authority continued to insist on the duty of people to obey—and argument had not yet swung round to the view that this duty arose from the fact that the laws were made by their own representatives. Law was to be obeyed because it was law, and without law there could be no liberty, no property, no society. But the inference was there for the taking: if the law failed to afford protection, if government failed to offer security, if in the long run it defaulted on the obligation of happiness, then the people's duty to support it would erode.[66]

Although this view of public order might seem theoretical, colonial America was not wanting in very practical demonstrations of a much more subversive kind. One of the most extreme was the great Massachusetts riot against British naval impressment in 1747. The popular reaction was the nearest thing to a general insurrection in New England until the Revolution, probably the nearest in all colonial history since Bacon's Rebellion in Virginia in 1676. Other instances, notably including the frontier rising and march of the Paxton boys in Pennsylvania in 1764, the New York land riots reflecting new rural radicalism in the Hudson Valley and land-hungry intrusions from Massachusetts in the mid-1760s, and the Regulator risings in both North and South Carolina later in that decade, were signs of a disposition—perhaps an increasing disposition—for men to take the remedy into their own hands when the institutions of lawful government either failed or obstructed them. Colonial governments, if they should be minded to hear the message, were receiving warnings that their obligations were not mere legal formalities. In the purely internal disturbances, both royal and proprietary governors were substantially aligned with the elected colonial representatives, and they interpreted their duty as being to restore order, where necessary by force. In the case of the naval riot, however, the royal authorities themselves appeared to the inhabitants as the chief threat to security and happiness; once the authority of the crown, acting through its multiplying agents in the colonies, took on this invidious role, the implications, though deeply disturbing, were increasingly difficult to resist.

In 1762 a furious dispute broke out in Massachusetts between the House of Representatives and Governor Francis Bernard, who had assumed responsibility for the operations of the province's only naval vessel, a sloop. The war with

France had not ceased, merchants wanted protection at sea, the assembly was in recess, and the governor took it as his duty in the interests of the province to keep the sloop in commission and send it out on active service. The trouble turned on a refined point of constitutional law. The sloop was paid for from public funds, raised—and therefore to be dispensed—only by the assembly's authority.

No one in Britain would have doubted the rightful power of the crown to act in the national defense. The House was therefore driving at a very significant distinction. In its view the crown's immediate agent in the province did not possess this prerogative power, which in effect had passed to the assembly through the principle of representative control over money raised by taxation. The House stated its position in a resolution which declared that this exertion of prerogative power by the royal governor was actually an act of *arbitrary* government. "No Necessity therefore," the House resolved, "can be sufficient to justify a house of Representatives in giving up such a Priviledge; for it would be of little consequence to the people whether they were subject to George or Lewis, the King of Great Britain or the French King, if both were arbitrary, as both would be if both could levy Taxes without Parliament." This language caused more than ordinary offense and on the governor's insistence was struck out; we have it from a pamphlet in which James Otis defended the House in terms almost equally provocative.[67] In the course of a stirring defense, Otis argued that "Kings were (and plantation governors should be) made for the good of the people, and not the people for them." It was also "humbly presumed that His Majesty would have the plantation governors follow his own example in strict adherence to the British Constitution." The position Otis had reached was nothing less, in its consequences, than that governments derived their legitimate right to govern by virtue of their effectiveness in protecting the rights and liberties of their subjects. In the context of the Enlightenment this theme would hardly be called extraordinary. But this was one of its earliest appearances in the more exacting context of relations between British authority and the elected representatives of a colony.

Five years later, after the Stamp Act and its repeal, after the passage of the Declaratory Act defining the full extent of parliamentary power over and in the colonies, and after the renewal of parliamentary levies on the colonies in the form of the Townshend tariffs, John Dickinson sat at his desk to compose his famous *Letters from a Farmer in Pennsylvania*, the first of which appeared in a Philadelphia newspaper in November 1767. Dickinson's *Letters* are of immense importance for understanding the developing colonial frame of mind. Within a few weeks almost every newspaper in the colonies had begun to reproduce either extracts or the full series of letters.[68] They did more than any other publication in these years to rally American sentiment, to unify opinion, and to demonstrate to people in the several colonies that they had a common cause. We can safely assume that Dickinson's main arguments were soon generally accepted and that they became highly representative.

Like Otis before him, Dickinson accepted the principle of the sovereignty of Parliament.[69] The colonies were but parts of a whole, and there must exist somewhere a power to preside and to preserve the parts in due order; and Dickinson agreed that this power was lodged in Parliament.[70] The fact that this was, by the time it was written, a conventional reason should not obscure the significance of the obvious: that it was a pragmatic reason. It was not based on constitutional law, still less on authoritarian principles such as might be derived from Britain's paternal relationship to the colonies; and it was totally devoid of divine right. But Dickinson then turned the course of the argument by alleging that the power claimed by Parliament—even by the Americans' supposed friend Pitt—would destroy American liberty and make Americans into as abject slaves as the peasants of France or Poland.[71]

Advancing a thesis of persuasive but deceptive moderation, Dickinson urged the value to the colonies of the connection with Britain, a point Otis had made a couple of years earlier. The prosperity of the colonies was founded on their dependence on Britain; but there was a corollary: "We have all the rights requisite for our prosperity."[72] It is not surprising that British observers had no difficulty in perceiving the subversive tendency at work in Dickinson's easy prose. For if the British connection should cease to be the best assurance of colonial prosperity the strongest reason advanced by Dickinson for maintaining the connection would lose its force. Allegiance to the throne itself was threatened by this pragmatic reasoning. It is true that he also adduced the ties of consanguinity, religion, and sentiment; but as he did so he clearly envisaged the possibility that the anguish of separation might have to be borne.

One year earlier, Dr. John Morgan, a medical professor at the College of Philadelphia, had offered a prize for essays on the "reciprocal advantages" of perpetual union between Britain and her colonies.[73] The prize essayists responded to this challenge as required by expounding the advantages to both sides, and it was in the very nature of the argument that they should dwell heavily on self-interest as the actuating force of politics. "Interest," said Joseph Reed, "becomes the grand prevailing principle that actuates all their—that is, each individual's—motives"; and commercial interest was the great object of the states of Europe. Another writer quoted Pope for the sentiment that "Self-love and social are the same."[74] Morgan himself wrote the leading contribution and stated that two thousand English ships were engaged each year in the American trade. The colonies derived from Britain their mild government, equal laws, and secure property.

Moving and convincing though these arguments may have been, they were fraught with the danger of rebound. For what would happen to the case for "perpetual union" if the Anglo-American connection ever ceased to serve American self-interest? Within a year of these events, Americans up and down the continent and in the British West Indies were raging that the government of Britain was harsh, not mild, that the laws imposed by her were unequal, and that this very dependence had rendered American property insecure.

To all the long series of American protests, British political spokesmen answered with arguments based on the absolute nature of parliamentary supremacy. Dickinson's words on this question were entirely British; in every body politic there must be some supreme and uncontrollable power; in the British Empire that power lay in Parliament. It could lie nowhere else. And the absence of such a power would be a certain recipe for disintegration. British administrators had never doubted this argument and had seldom if ever relied on any other. All of the many attempts made earlier in the century by the Board of Trade to reorganize the empire and bring it under tighter and more efficient control; the manuscript dissertations written in 1752 and 1774 by the well-informed administrator James Abercromby, urging on his masters a complete reconstruction of the imperial system; the treatises and memorandums of William Knox, another administrator who, like Abercromby, had experience of the colonies, as well as innumerable parliamentary speeches and pronouncements down to the beginnings of the final crisis, all rested on parliamentary sovereignty.[75] It was not indeed the only thesis to reinforce British authority. In the heat of the quarrel this legal basis was backed by a strong and openly authoritarian form of paternalism. Britain to the colonies stood in the relation of parent to child; both gratitude and filial piety commanded due obedience.[76]

So long as no one in any responsible position on either side could doubt that the colonies and Britain were in truth members of a single community, the argument held together; Americans had no wish to supersede the theory of sovereignty, and none of them proposed an alternative. Only a very few of them seem to have had any wish to displace the Parliament of Great Britain, which clearly stood at the center of a vast network that no other authority could hope to control. But subversive agents were at work, and they burrowed from the interior of the argument. The very definition of community had become infected with pragmatic considerations of interest; and the most effective parts of the argument, on both sides, had passed into a mode that was essentially utilitarian. Not utilitarian, perhaps, in the strict sense of the greatest happiness of the greatest number, but in the sense of applying pragmatic tests of utility to rules prescribed on the basis of will and superiority. And once the test of utility was applied to the particular acts of Parliament, it was sure soon to be applied to the British Empire itself.

Most American commentators were lawyers, and, as Bernard Bailyn has observed, their arguments were intensely legalistic. A similar observation was made at the time by Edmund Burke: "In no country, perhaps, is law so general a study."[77] They sought to persuade by force of legal reasoning, and when that failed, by appeals to the equal rights of British subjects. These in fact were often two branches of the same argument. But the British laws under question were challenged for attacking rights, and these were rights *in* something; in other words, they were expressions of interests, a concept which colonists, like their British counterparts, had spent nearly a lifetime getting to know, understand, and use. Americans responded to these British laws in the way they did because they received them in a frame of mind that had become permeated with utilitarian precepts about the nature and significance of interests; and once the imperial government had ceased to provide the conditions of Americans' happiness, it began to relax its legitimate claim on their loyalty.

The British colonial administrator William Knox wrote a memorandum in 1778 or 1779 analyzing the reasons for the revolt. He listed the "predominancy of the Democratic power" in colonial governments, the inattention and incapacity of those charged with colonial administration in the home government, and, above all, the failure of the British policy makers to provide the colonists with constitutions that would have assured them of safeguards for their rights and property similar to those of British subjects at home.[78] Burke, who, as a member of the Rockingham party, was to some extent handicapped by his adherence to the Declaratory Act, got at the core of the matter in his great speech on conciliation with the colonies in 1775. Burke was anxious to avoid fine questions of constitutional law, which he regarded as standing in the way of practical compromises. He offered his solution in terms of interests. "My idea, without considering whether we yield as a matter of right, or grant as a matter of favour, is to admit the people of our colonies into an interest in the constitution; and, by recording that interest in the journals of parliament, to give them as strong an assurance as the nature of the thing will admit, that we mean forever to adhere to that solemn declaration of systematick indulgence."[79] In the nature of British constitutional development, such an act or declaration would gradually come to have been accepted as having constitutional status, and in the course of time the Declaratory Act would have become obsolete. In the existing state of opinion, however, other ways had to be found of achieving the same ultimate object.

Looking back, then, over the period that begins with the Restoration and ends with the American Revolution, we can discern a transition from a theory of government sustained at least in part by some form of divine right to a theory which makes the very authority of government depend on the utilitarian test of its ability to protect and promote interests. As another expression of the same process, government loses its mission to maintain a given religious system and acquires the still more troublesome burden of creating—or protecting—

the conditions in which the people are happy. When government itself violates these conditions, it falls by its own motion. In such circumstances we can perhaps consider the language of contract, which had played a pivotal part in justifying the resistance since the Glorious Revolution, as a metaphor which had the merit of satisfying men's desire for legal sanction.

By the time of the first Continental Congress, in September 1774, American leaders were willing to incorporate an appeal to natural rights into the legalistic weave of their argument.[80] Natural rights may be described as the divine rights of common people; a king who was reduced to appealing to natural rights would not be in a strong position. Jeremy Bentham, who considered himself the founder of the utilitarian system, described natural rights as "simple nonsense" and "natural and imprescriptible rights" as "rhetorical nonsense—nonsense upon stilts." The harm he saw in this style of talk was that these rights were at once translated into legal rights.[81] This was not a view that would have been kindly received in America, where natural rights were gaining a status superior to those attaching to constitutional law. But if we look searchingly enough into the natural rights argument adopted by Americans, we shall find that Bentham might have been reconciled to them after all. For the test of natural rights was utilitarian satisfaction.

Lord North was gradually moved by the force of events. In the spring of 1775, and then some three years later, he offered constitutional concessions to the American Congress, and although he failed to impress that body, he did at least prove a philosophical point. To justify any further claim to American allegiance, the British government was obliged to guarantee to protect colonial happiness and to refrain from encroaching on the rights which protected that condition. But the British had been wielding a weapon that broke in their hands; and colonial leaders no longer trusted them. To prove their own point, the colonists took up arms and, with French help, won the war.

The irony of history turns more often on the victors than on the vanquished. Long before the end of the war, the Americans were forced to take over the responsibilities which the British had so long and so laboriously tried to discharge. In this process, American governments soon discovered that they had to impose on their peoples the most extensive, intrusive, and detailed system of government that any of them had ever experienced.

CHAPTER TWO

The Crown
in the Colonies

B ritain's colonies owed their existence to men and women who were ready to emigrate to improve their fortunes or to save their souls. But they owed their legal authority as corporate bodies and their claim to protection when occupying distant territories to the charters they received from the hands of the crown. Only in the late case of Georgia, founded in 1732, did Parliament take any part in the process by which a British colony was formed; the Georgia Trustees were established by Parliament, and their status was subject to parliamentary review. The charter itself, of course, flowed from the crown. Earlier parliaments did not have this opportunity to share in the founding of a colony, and it is doubtful whether any earlier parliament would have wished to do so. The exception, therefore, is significant by its date. A change was taking place in the contribution of Parliament to the government of Britain, and that change was eventually transmitted to and felt by the colonies no less than within the realm.

So little part did any conception of parliamentary sovereignty play in the early years that after the execution of Charles I the Virginia House of Burgesses, at the instigation of the Cavalier Governor William Berkeley, declared its allegiance to Charles II—which, in the circumstances existing in England, left the Virginians in a state of virtual autonomy. It was only in 1652 that Cromwell's Parliament reduced Virginia to formal submission, and then on terms which Massachusetts could not have improved on. The government was to remain in the hands of the General Assembly, no taxes were to be raised, nor were any forts to be built or garrisons maintained in the province without its consent: home rule remained where home rule mattered—over finance and military power.[1] These terms would have left the parliaments of the next century with very little room for maneuver if they had been able to survive the Commonwealth. But they were agreed upon by a regicide government, and their entire claim to legal status collapsed on the Restoration. Within Virginia it may have seemed that very little had changed, but the province had reverted to its former status as a royal colony.

Massachusetts Bay's antagonism to royal authority was more explicit and troublesome, so much so that a formal demand for the surrender of the charter was made as early as 1638— a demand the colony's rulers rejected, in an early display of the temper that was to prove characteristic.[2] Charles I very soon had other things to think about, and the question was allowed to lapse. Complaints against religious discrimination became much more active and organized in the 1640s, and the leading dissident, Robert Child, expressed his grievances to the House of Commons, an action which the Bay authorities regarded as little short of treason. But by that time the House contained many members who were sympathetic to the Puritan experiment; the situation did not seem to call for parliamentary intervention, and the occasion was hardly suitable. But the government of Charles II, once settled on the throne, could not ignore complaints of discrimination against members of the Church of England nor the evidence of calculated disregard for English authority. In 1664 the king dispatched a royal commission to investigate the recalcitrant colony.

The commission, which encountered almost every variety of noncooperation and obstruction short of guerrilla warfare,

eventually succeeded in bringing about certain limited reforms. The suffrage was redefined to permit nonmembers of
the Congregational churches to vote provided they met property qualifications, which were in any case conventional. But
the colony's ability to assert its independence had proved almost a match for the powers of the crown. The continuing
disputes between the English and colonial authorities did not
arise from mere waywardness but from a very manifest conviction that Massachusetts was in many respects actually outside the crown's jurisdiction. When, in 1676, Edward Randolph
was sent out with a commission to enforce the navigation
laws, the difference was dramatized on the very day of his
arrival. With a royal proclamation in his hand, Randolph removed his hat, a symbolic acknowledgment of the presence
of the sovereign. But while three councillors removed their
hats, the governor of Massachusetts-Bay and three members
of the council remained covered.[3]

No other act of symbolic defiance could have more clearly
demonstrated the claim for quasi-autonomy. But from a later
standpoint, the incident at least narrows and concentrates the
focus of the dispute. The crown had sent the royal instructions; and this act of contempt—or nonrecognition, which
where crowns are concerned amounts to very much the same
thing—was directed at the crown. The whole of New England's dispute was with the crown. Although the Navigation
Act was itself the work of Parliament, it was the crown which
created the Committee on Plantations selected in 1675 from
members of the Privy Council; all its members sat by royal
appointment. Without the authority and action of the crown,
the act would have no force. The crown was also the source
of the move in the late 1670s to introduce into Jamaica and
Virginia the law which for centuries had governed the constitutional status of Ireland. (This step encountered strong
resistance and was abandoned for a favorable compromise on
the grant of a permanent revenue in Jamaica; it was with-

drawn for less clear reasons in Virginia).[4] When in due course—there could be few to doubt that it was due course—James II proceeded by way of legal action against the charter of Massachusetts, the case lay between the crown and the colony.

The point may seem to need little emphasis. It would certainly have been obvious at the time but acquires its distinctiveness from a long subsequent history which contemporaries did not live to see. The destruction of the New England charters, followed by the establishment of the Dominion of New England (including New York) together constituted the first wave of English policies which most New Englanders regarded as a form of oppression. Possessing a superiority of local force, they rose up and overturned the government of the royal agent in their midst—encouraged by tidings of what they believed to be the example of a greater but similar rebellion in England. A long lifetime later, the descendants of these local rebels encountered a second great wave of oppression, which began after the defeat of France in the Seven Years' War. But that later wave was an entirely different affair, not only in its motives and aims but in the authority on which it was based. The Revenue Act of 1764, the Stamp Act, the Townshend Tariff Act, and in 1774 the so-called "Intolerable Acts" all required the royal assent to make them valid; but they were acts of Parliament and represented the fullest possible claim of absolute authority over the empire. That claim was affirmed in uncompromising language in the Declaratory Act of 1766, an act that did not claim to *make* law, but merely to declare what the law was and had always been. In short, over a period of some eighty years, there had been a decisive transition from a form of imperial government based on the crown to a form which claimed its authority from Parliament.

To these parliamentary assertions the colonies could not reply with a single voice and mind. It was at first very difficult to separate their natural and widespread dislike of what was happening from their constitutional reasons for objecting to

45

parliamentary taxation. The problems were genuinely diffi-cult, the boundaries elusive. After all, the colonies had never previously objected that parliamentary taxes imposed to reg-ulate imperial trade were invalid, and the Molasses Act of 1733 was ignored rather than challenged. It remained until the last extremely difficult to define the colonies out of the range of the navigation laws, which they had always ac-cepted; but the logic of the arguments that were gaining ground in the colonies nevertheless pointed in precisely that direc-tion. When this theme had been fully worked out, the effect was to return the colonies full circle to the early position of sole allegiance to the crown. Parliament had ceased to occupy a legitimate place in their scheme of government. And it was this position which in its turn enabled them to denounce the king and to renounce their allegiance to him on the ground that he had violated the "contract" supposed to exist between crown and subjects. This view of the relationship derived di-rectly from the language adopted by the English Convention Parliament of 1689 and owed much of its moral authority to the political writings of John Locke.

But this view of the relationship raised a question which colonial leaders—who were also in most cases the principal theoreticians—no longer had time to answer. If it were cor-rect, one could legitimately ask where Parliament had come from and how the colonial assemblies had interpreted its role in their lives during the long period in which its authority appeared to have been accepted.

This question opens a path of inquiry which historians have not generally chosen to explore. This indifference must be partly explained by the extraordinary sparsity of comment on the Glorious Revolution, and more particularly on its signifi-cance for the colonies, in the records of colonial political dis-course. If it is always difficult to wring meaning from silence, it is important to realize that the silence is part of the problem. The silence must be interrogated in the context of the sounds that surround it.

Our basic question can be stated as that of what politically minded colonists *thought* had happened in the Glorious Revolution. The problem is inherently confusing. There is no clear and simple answer, and there was no clear answer in 1689. No Englishman at that date knew or guessed at the solutions that would be hammered out through the furious controversies of the reigns of William and Mary and of Anne. Neither did the Dutch Prince of Orange, now become King William III. It is not surprising that at different periods during the next seventy years, different colonial legislatures often gave different answers: the lack of any coherent comprehension is part of the answer. Nor do I think any good purpose will be served by reopening the question of legal right and wrong.[5] The problem is rather to try to satisfy ourselves as to how the people on either side of this prolonged and formidable struggle came to hold the convictions which at length drove them to oppose each other in a British civil war. If they were to control the courses of their own lives, they had to respond to them according to their own interpretations. How, then, did they acquire those interpretations? It seems to me to be a very important if somewhat taken-for-granted attribute of American public psychology—and had been so from the first migrations—that as emigrants and as colonials, people did want to control their own lives. The act of emigration was itself a potent manifestation of this awakening desire among the people of Europe. These people were not content to be passengers or galley slaves on someone else's transport through life.

The question we are asking is essentially a question in history rather than in law or logic. It is no part of my own intention that this inquiry should cast one beam of light so intense and consuming as to clear up all remaining doubts and, in the process, wither up all previous interpretations. I do, however, hope to make the views of the colonists more intelligible by suggesting explanations as to why they came to see the problems they confronted in the way they did; and in that context I hope to show that the problem of coping with Parliament was not only a difficult challenge in terms of constitutional principles but that the difficulty arose in part because, in the form taken in the eighteenth century, it was also a novel problem.

In tracing the threads that connect the American mind of 1689 with that of the revolutionary era, I propose to take as a point of departure an easily ascertained but generally unnoticed date. It may or may not be a fact that John Dickinson finished the first of his *Farmer's Letters* on 5 November 1767. It is a fact, and a signal, an exercise in ideological semiotics, that he placed that date at the foot of his first essay. None of his readers was expected to miss the point, but for safety's sake he added a footnote and a subsequent reference in the text to remind them that 5 November was the date of the Prince of Orange's landing at Torbay in 1688.[6] The protest of 1767 was thus placed firmly on the basis of the values that Dickinson drew from the Glorious Revolution. But if at the same time his protest was directed against the policies of Parliament, we may legitimately ask how Dickinson himself conceived of parliamentary power. But Dickinson did not directly engage this question. By reaching straight back to the Revolution itself, he was able to evade the problem of how Parliament had acquired and exercised its imperial powers; it was enough to maintain that if Parliament used its powers to contravene the values of the Revolution, that exercise was illegitimate and might in the last resort force the injured party to the remedies adopted by the English nation in 1688.

Increase Mather, who had gone to England in Massachusetts's cause before the fall of Andros, was better placed than most of his countrymen to perceive that the legislative power exercised by Parliament in England was likely to have its bearing on his own colony. William's first intention, on the advice of his Privy Council, had been to retain the Dominion structure for the government of New England; it was the rebellion in Boston that made them think again.[7] Parliament might thus have a part to play in saving New England from continued despotism; and it was surely fit and proper that a parliament composed of the men who had rescued England should apply the same principles to New England. Thus in a pamphlet he published in London early in 1689, Mather expressed the hope that "His Majesty and the High Court of Parliament, will put that value upon New England, as so vast a Tract of Land and Body of People [he had put their numbers at two hundred thousand] deserve from a Government on which they depend, and are so great and useful a Member, as they have manifested themselves to be."[8] A Boston broadsheet "Published to prevent false Reports" indicated that all was going well "in Parliament and at Court"; New England's interests were being cared for, and the writer of a letter from London thought the charter would be restored by Parliament.[9] The idea here was that the original charter would be given back. Since Parliament had just installed a new king and queen to restore England's ancient constitution, there was nothing to fear from a parliamentary grant, or regrant, of the charter. This was the nation's true Parliament, arising from true English principles of government and religion.

Mather's first step had been to appeal directly to James II, who was attempting to rally support from the religious opposites of English life, the Catholics and the Dissenting Protestants. But the king's flight simplified Mather's position. For a short period he pinned his hope on a bill before Parliament to restore all the corporation charters that had been struck down since the Restoration, and he helped to shape this bill to include the colonies. Whether or not Parliament had a legal right to intervene in charters given by the king was a question as yet untested. But the result of some intensive concentration on the question of the colonies was to convince William that they were part of his personal possessions and must be placed under royal control. Mather accordingly swung his attentions sharply back to the court; and it seems to have been the king himself who decided on the basic form of the new government. The providential blessing Mather could bring back to his ungrateful countrymen was a restored representative assembly; the countervailing price, however, was a permanent royal presence in the person of the governor. One effect was to institutionalize, even to polarize, the pulling power of the crown as against that of the people of the colony; and there seemed every likelihood that the crown would have an invincible advantage. Nevertheless, Mather, more than his unwelcome colleagues in London, saw the vital importance of accepting this gift from the crown. Worse had been known, and Mather was well placed to appreciate that worse might easily have followed. He seems to have expected to negotiate like an emissary from a quasi-independent power, in return for which presumption he was brutally told in Whitehall that the colonists' consent was neither expected nor desired.[10]

New England's inclination was undoubtedly to go straight back to its direct relation to the crown, insofar as that was a necessary condition of charter government. If parliamentary intervention proved unavoidable, the best thing to do was to live in the faith that Parliament was benign. But it would on the whole be better if Parliament had nothing to do with the matter. The danger was that too many New Englanders might come to regard even the crown connection as a formality. Gershom Bulkeley therefore wrote to dissuade his Connecticut fellow countrymen from holding elections until authority came from England because he feared they would get a reputation for being ungovernable; in the absence of a charter, there was no formal government, but he was at pains to deny that this state of affairs meant that *no* government existed in the province. "The Governor is not the head of the government," he explained, "but the *King*: And the government is not his property originally but the *king's*." The governor was only the king's minister. "It would not do for us to anticipate new orders from the Crown of England."[11] Bulkeley's own conservative temperament no doubt disposed him toward an appreciation of the risks involved. But his emphasis on the direct power of the crown was important, because Connecticut's quasi-independent status had not saved it from being unceremoniously reorganized into the Dominion by order of King James II. Here as in Massachusetts the main emphasis was on dependence on the Crown—a dependence even Increase Mather had expressly admitted. In general, with the exceptions noted, the literature surrounding the uprising had no occasion to dwell on Parliament; if Parliament, in the extraordinary circumstances of the time, could play a part in getting the charter restored, that was not to be considered as a wedge by which it would play itself into the government of New England. The charter was and would remain a royal instrument. In 1718 a royal official was told, "Acts of Parliament have no force with us, for we have a charter."[12]

If these feelings centered round the charter in Massachusetts and Connecticut, they were hardly less significant in New York. The printed books of laws began in 1691 with a "magna charta or fundamental constitution" under which "the kings of England only" were invested with the right to rule. Beneath them came the governor—a royal appointment—the council and the elected representatives of the people. There was no mention of Parliament, not because of any express desire to repudiate parliamentary authority, but more simply because it had never been present and had no part in either the sources of authority or the structure of the colony's government.[13]

Events in subsequent years did very little to alter this state of affairs. New York's Leislerian party succeeded in getting Parliament to reverse Jacob Leisler's attainder, an incident which established a tentative affinity between them and the English Whigs.[14] This, however, was an exercise of exceptional power. The attainder and execution of Leisler took place in abnormal circumstances, and it is doubtful whether the Privy Council would have permitted a colonial government to exercise such power at any other time. This exception serves to illustrate the absence of the parliamentary arm from the legislative life of the colonies. The most distinct exercise of Parliament's authority in the colonies occurred in 1710, when a continental post office was established as part of an extensive law providing for British postal service.[15] This was certainly an act of Parliament reaching into the colonies and could be cited in later years as evidence that colonial legislatures had not objected to the principle of legislation. But this was another exception. No colonial legislature could have organized or authorized an intercolonial service of this kind; only Parliament possessed either the authority or in the practical sense the ability to make a collective provision for the colonies. The act constitutes a good precedent for parliamentary authority over the empire as a whole but by the same token a weak precedent for parliamentary legislation reaching the internal affairs of the colonies.

When the news reached Boston in 1702 that William III's hardworking life had come to an end, Increase Mather delivered an important sermon. He dedicated it to Governor Joseph Dudley, recently appointed by the late king. Mather lamented that the king's death had "made way for great calamities to break in upon the *Protestant Churches*. If they are in a flame, will not some of the sparks fly over to *New England*? *New England* could not have lost a better friend. How often have I heard very kind expressions concerning his subjects in New England proceed out of that royal mouth, which I cannot now think of without bleeding sorrow."[16] Later in the sermon Mather returned to the king to remind his audience that "when God made him our King he was the great Instrument delivering us from popery and Slavery."[17] William was praised for his part in consenting to acts of Parliament for the liberty of the subject as had never been passed before and for helping to restore civil as well as religious liberties.[18] Civil liberties had thus entered into the canon of virtues that Massachusetts was dedicated to sustain. This was more than eulogy; it was politics. When Mather insisted that his fellow countrymen ought to be grateful for "the great privileges our present Charter confirms"—adding ominously that "if we are not, our friends in England will not think we deserve more" and that "We must also use our privileges well"—he was defending his own record as the chief negotiator who had conceded the charter's terms in Whitehall and who had brought the new document back to a skeptical province.[19] The hostility it there encountered had never wholly subsided.

It was natural on this occasion that Mather should emphasize the crown. Parliament got a look in when he mentioned that William had given his assent to its acts, but even here it was the king who got most of the credit. But even aside from the king's death, the emphasis was wholly in keeping with the existing situation so far as it affected the colonies, and more particularly Massachusetts with its new royal charter. His enemies might think his expressions too fulsome, but Mather had better reason to know from the very tough negotiations he had carried through in London that the relationship of colonies to the imperial power was a dependent one. The wars with France had recently forced New England into a closer connection with the mother country than ever before; even the people of Massachusetts were beginning to recognize advantages in British protection.[20] Mather was also better placed than most of his countrymen to know that they might not have seen the last of English attempts to reorganize the colonies. During the war that ended with the Peace of Utrecht in 1713, five bills were introduced into Parliament with a view to making all the proprietary and charter colonies dependent on the crown.[21]

It was comforting, and sometimes useful, to have allies in both houses of Parliament. But anyone engaged in promoting colonial interests knew that the main business had to be done with officials who, whichever board they belonged to, owed their appointments primarily to the crown. Nor did this situation alter with the transition from the last of the Stuarts, in the person of Queen Anne, to the first of the Hanovers. King George I's attorney general gave it as his opinion that the crown, by means of instruction, had power to alter both the qualifications of colonial electors and the means of election.[22] No parliament ever claimed such powers until, by implication, the Declaratory Act of 1766; but no parliament made any attempt to exercise them until the Massachusetts Government Act, which reconstituted the province's government in 1774. From the standpoint of the early eighteenth century, this later assertion of parliamentary power not only over but within the colonies would have seemed revolutionary.

Massachusetts was not the only grumbling province. Many among New York's very mixed population had no British roots and no particular reason to feel affection for or affinity with Britain. Governor the Earl of Bellomont detected "Faction and Sedition," which had "taken root" in the town. He rebuked these murmurings in a strong speech delivered in 1699 to the new assembly, elected after he had dismissed the old one for inactivity. "And there has been the utmost industry us'd by some ill Men to spread the Infection all over the Province, and to alienate the Affections of the People by false suggestions and Notions of their Independance [sic] of the crown of *England*, and that 'tis a Violence and Wrong done 'em that *England* should put a limitation on their Trade. How extravagant and wild is this Notion," he continued; "does not England put a restriction on its own Trade, in some Cases?" He then launched his attack on piracy, rife in New York but held in abomination in England. Back to the main theme, he insisted, "People must not be deceived, this Province is subject to the Crown of *England*; and it is its greatest Glory and Happiness that it is so." It was this that entitled them to the protection of the crown. It also gave them the best constitution of laws and the advantage of fellowship with the people of England—"the best and bravest people in the World." It was their duty and interest to be obedient to English laws.[23]

To judge by Bellomont's personal opinions, these laws were not likely to be seen at their best in the hands of New York's lawyers. "As to the men that call themselves lawyers here and practice at the bar, they are almost all under such a scandalous character, that it would grieve a man to see our noble English laws so miserably mangled profaned. . . . So far from being barristers, one of them was a dancing master; another a glover by trade; a third, which is Mr. Jamison, was condemned to be hanged in Scotland for burning the Bible and for blasphemy. . . . Besides their ignorance in the law, they are all, except one or two, violent enemies to the government, and they do a world of mischief in the country by infecting the people with ill principles toward the government."[24]

The two critical themes here are similar to those in New England. First, the colonies owed allegiance to the crown. Obedience to the laws—parliamentary enactments—followed from that allegiance. The situation was particularly difficult for Bellomont because his predecessor, Benjamin Fletcher, had taken sides with the anti-Leislerian faction and was accused of having encouraged and profited from piracy, not a good example of law enforcement to come from the chief officer of the province. But disaffection clearly went deeper than that. Below the level of official discourse, the grumblings of resentment to be heard in Massachusetts by those who took the trouble to listen were disturbingly similar.

General underlying hostility to royal government was sharpened by the enforcement of the British policy of reserving the best pines for mastwood for the Royal Navy. In 1722 or 1723 Lord Carteret, as secretary of state with charge of the colonies, sent out a personal agent whose observations told more than could have been gathered from many governors' formal reports. Once he got among the people, this agent heard no more of the artificial deference that decorated the resolutions of the assembly. His Majesty had "no business in this country"; he was only "our nominal king." It was murmured that "the Country is ours not his. . . . The King or his Governour has no power to doe us either good or hurt." Addresses of loyalty were a sham, blindfolding the commissioners of trade, "so that the true state of this country has never been yet knowen to H.M. or his Ministers, but all huddled upon secrecy and juggle." He also reported barbarous treatment of Indians, many of whom had been burned alive in a barn, others sold as slaves. There was dangerous discontent among the blacks; Negro slaves had raised fires in Boston. It is clear that when he got back to Boston himself, he thought the governor should be given some account of his impressions, but both the governors and the judges assured him that these "treasonable speeches" of which he complained were "the comon dialect of the country, which they were glad to suffer for fear of their resentment, etc."[25]

Carteret's agent did not believe that soldiers could suppress these attitudes. Instead he outlined a scheme of his own to raise a rent from all the colonies. But he concluded his report on a note of profound skepticism: "If any man offers to drink H.M.'s health we call it Popry and him a Papist, and we sing a requiem to ourselves for the death of K"—presumably meaning King George.[26] Reviewing this evidence, Cecil Headlam, the editor of these volumes of the *Calendar of State Papers*, observed, "The state of opinion, in fact, so far as Massachusetts was concerned, was not far different now [in 1723] from that which prevailed in the American Revolution. What was different was the presence at the earlier period of the danger from the French and Indians, the political and financial position of Great Britain, and the actions of the British Government as influenced by it."[27]

For open political purposes, the opposition, whether loyal or disloyal, was obliged to accept the constitutional facts of life in a crown colony. Some of the expressions reported may have amounted to no more than an extreme example of the Englishman's right to grumble. No one would publicly claim more than a moral entitlement to the province's original charter rights. But it was this that caused such recurrent resentment against the second charter, which became the focus of a new dispute, dating from the regime of Governor Samuel Shute and coming to a head under Lieutenant-Governor William Dummer in the mid-1720s.

Shute claimed the power to appoint the attorney general, which the assembly angrily contested. He then, in 1720, vetoed the assembly's choice of Speaker and resolved the deadlock by dissolving the session.[28] Since the charter left these powers undefined, Shute had no doubt that they belonged to the governor as part of the prerogative. But over the question of the speakership he was certainly claiming for himself as royal governor more than the crown would have claimed in England, and it is far from surprising that a representative body, which was developing the habit of comparing itself to the House of Commons, should have challenged the claim. The right to dissolve the legislature, on the other hand, was a normal executive power, though its exercise was certainly an abrupt intrusion into the assembly's normal conduct of business.

The controversy passed to the Privy Council, another reminder to Massachusetts that it did not control the ultimate interpretation of its own charter—but a reminder to us, incidentally, that it was the crown and not Parliament that determined the status of colonial governments. The Privy Council might have taken advantage of the opportunity to review the charter as a whole and clearly kept that possibility in mind; but instead it narrowed the issue to the two points of contention, in both of which it declared in the governor's favor. The resulting instrument was called the Explanatory Charter.

When this instrument came before the General Court in

1726, that body was given the unusual option of accepting or rejecting a document officially emanating from the king. The strenuous opposition it encountered there is the more remarkable in view of the obvious danger that a rejection would have given the British authorities occasion to recall the existing charter and write a new one. Whether this argument helped to overcome the objections of the assembly is unknown. In due course, with evident bad grace, the Explanatory Charter was accepted by forty-eight votes to thirty-two, and Lieutenant Governor Dummer reported soothingly but misleadingly to the Council of Trade and Plantations that "The General Assembly have dutyfully accepted H.M. Royal Explanatory Charter a copy of their vote for the same is herewith enclosed."[29]

The force of the formal opposition is one significant lesson of this episode. When thirty-two members of the House of Representatives, including all of Boston's delegation, were prepared to oppose acceptance of a royal instrument and to take the risk of a major constitutional crisis, they can only have spoken for a formidable body of discontent. It is true that the issue, especially that of the governor's veto of the Speaker, concerned the extent of the House's powers; and Massachusetts was not accustomed to accepting defeats. A reasonable man of the province, weighing the issue, might well have concluded that some portion of traditional freedom was at stake. Others could as well have concluded that this portion could naturally be claimed by the governor, that it was in the nature of the colonial relationship. One is forced to the inference that a large body of the politically minded men of Massachusetts really did not like that degree of dependency.

A second lesson, because more obvious, is easier to overlook. In the context of the argument that I am developing, however, it will be clear that this very positive intervention in the distribution of the internal governmental powers of the province was an act of the executive, not of the legislature. The significance of this point is not diminished by the fact that Parliament had begun to extend its policies of regulating colonial trade; the trade and navigation laws were assuming a complexity and extent that inevitably reached into colonial life, and Parliament was soon to reach still further, restraining the colonists from producing beaver hats or producing iron goods for intercolonial sale. In a legal sense, these restrictions all pertained to a specific and limited area of British national life—its overseas economy. Since a family's livelihood then as now depended on economic activities, and since livelihood determined a great deal about the style of life available, it would not have required much perspicuity to demonstrate that Parliament was really touching many of the details of colonial lives. It was, moreover, the English Act of Toleration of 1689 which now represented official British policy toward a stubbornly reluctant Massachusetts. In this instance the English authorities had seized the opportunity of writing essential provisions into the new charter—a restriction Connecticut escaped. Yet it was still true that parliamentary interventions were rare, limited, and specific; Parliament did not draw up the instructions to royal governors, made no colonial appointments, did not lay down or alter the structure of colonial governments or judiciaries, and did not lay internal taxes on the colonies. Forty years later, Parliament was to assert its power to legislate for the colonies "in all cases whatsoever."[30] No occasion for a declaratory act had arisen at any previous period, nor were the exact powers of Parliament ever clearly defined. But it is doubtful whether Parliament would in fact have wished to make such absolute claims in the first half of the century.[31]

In its frequent quarrels with royal governors, Massachusetts continued through its official declarations and political pamphleteers to emphasize its fundamental connections with the crown. Elisha Cooke—the elected Speaker whom Shute rejected—published a statement in his own defense in which he denied charges of having invaded the king's rights in the woods of Maine. Cooke argued the rights of the House of Representatives from the language of the charter and declared his loyalty to King George, the prince of "our Nation." Whether the nation was Britain and its colonies considered as a whole, or whether this was a case in which Massachusetts men were expected to consider themselves a nation under the king, was discreetly left to the speculation of a local audience.[32] When William Burnet, son of the famous Whig bishop, became governor, the salary squabble was soon resumed. A pamphleteer replied to the argument that the House of Representatives had too much power by referring to the danger of unlimited monarchy as in France. Happily, there was no need to enter into this question under the king, who, like his father, "is universally acknowledged to make the known Laws the Rule, and his People's Happiness, the End of his Government." There had been no fears on this account since the accession of King William. It was an argument that subtly linked the principle that the happiness of the people was the object of government with the line of monarchs since the Glorious Revolution.[33] The same theme was expounded before the newly arrived Governor Burnet in a sermon by Thomas Prince, who was at pains to distinguish between English corporations and the charter of New England. The former, he declared, were acts of grace; but he now hooked the theory of contract into the history of the royal charter with the assertion that the charter was a contract between the king and the first patentees. This was a statement that would certainly have caused great surprise to King Charles I, who had never heard of contracts between kings and their subjects and would not have issued a charter if any such suggestion had been made. Prince, however, took particular advantage of the governor's parentage to establish a connection which linked the rights secured by the Glorious Revolution to those originally granted by Charles I.[34]

This argument, which appears to have required some intellectual ingenuity, in fact took up the theme that the original settlers had been serving the king's interests by enlarging his dominions, which had been first heard in the pamphlets justifying the revolt against Andros. The idea of describing the charter as a contract was a development that had been available only since the Revolution of 1688–89, and it incorporated the English theory of the Revolution with the normal and previous status of Massachusetts in a way that goes far to explain why the Glorious Revolution plays so little part in the subsequent political polemics of the colonies. The Revolution originated no rights; it confirmed what they already knew and furnished them with additional ammunition, made the more potent by its place in the sources of English constitutional doctrine.

When the General Court returned to the salary issue after greeting Burnet, it extended its traditional claim to the rights of Englishmen by a new argument: the assembly claimed credit for maintaining the balance of the constitution.[35] This could only mean that the constitution of Massachusetts rested on exactly the same principles as that of England. When the Privy Council sustained Burnet, the House chose to interpret the decision as giving them a choice of whether or not to vote financial support for their governor. In the long run the assembly got its way. Burnet did not live to press his case, and his successors preferred to accommodate. The House of Representatives had risked a serious collision with Walpole's administration and had correctly sensed that the springs of power, so supple at home, would not be tightened in the colonies.[36]

By this time, we can observe a profound shift in the character of Massachusetts opposition since the Andros crisis. Before Andros, the justifications that had periodically to be offered for the colony's waywardness were found in the high motives and heroic sacrifices of the early settlers; their inspiration was religious, but their enterprise brought benefit to the crown. But by the 1720s and 1730s, the official assembly position, sharpened in repeatedly renewed disputes with the governor, had become a conventional English appeal to rights that were constitutional because the colonists were English. Even the conventional balance of the constitution had been invoked. All this was accompanied by fervent denials that they aimed at anything so wild as "independency"—denials directed at the evident suspicions of the Lords of Trade.[37]

The element known in assembly politics as the Country party, led by Elisha Cooke, Jr., son of the original enemy of the Charter of 1691, had long been a recognized force. This is not to say that it had much to oppose in the ordinary business of government or even that it conspired to make life difficult for royal governors when constitutional questions were not at stake. But it did tend to seek opportunities to extend the range of the assembly's powers and to find constitutional issues where no one had looked for them before. The outcry over the commissioning by Governor Bernard of the province sloop, undertaken for purposes of mercantile defense, which took place some thirty years later, can only be considered as evidence that through the years of war in the mid-century period this tendency had not disappeared but, on the contrary, under determined leadership had grown more extreme.

The many phases of that long period produced ups and downs in the relationship between the House and the governors. When Jonathan Belcher was appointed, the Country party sought an alliance with him and suddenly became the court.[38] But there is persistent evidence for the existence of an underground level of slightly mutinous opposition. Much the same may be said for other provinces. When in the mid-1740s William Douglass came to compose his history of the British settlements, he reached conclusions about the mentality of the common people which could hardly have been of comfort to those who looked for eternal loyalty to the empire, all the more because it was reflected in conspicuous aspects of policy adopted by elected colonial leaders. As a result of mankind's natural desire for "parity and leveling, without any fixed superiority," Douglass observed, not only Connecticut and Rhode Island, but some of the proprietary governments, "are of opinion, that they are not obliged to attend to, or follow, any instructions or orders from their *mother-country* or court of *Great-Britain*; they do not send their laws home to the plantation-offices to be presented to the King-in-council for approbation or disallowance." On the other hand, like all colonial writers, he was careful to disavow any inclination to withdraw from dependence on Britain.[39]

The picture of the political society of much of the colonies that emerges from these observations suggests the existence of turbulent forces, which often disturbed and sometimes pierced the formal crust of colonial society. This crust of men engaged in public life, and also, frequently, in those more advanced forms of the economic life which connected their colonies with the transatlantic world, formally acknowledged and worked with the agencies of British sovereignty. They learned the rules of the games of imperial politics, knew how to manipulate them—sometimes to the disadvantage of royal officials—and either operated or subverted them with about equal degrees of loyalty to the empire. Beyond the empire they did not look. For the most part, and most of the time, it must be said that the mass of the people deferentially accepted their places in a world in which their primary task was to make a living. They needed the stability given by good government, with firm, experienced, and knowledgeable leadership. But there was among them less, and perhaps a diminishing, attachment to the British people and nation. The Earl of Loudoun, commander-in-chief of forces in North America in 1756, reported to the Earl of Halifax at the Board of Trade that this form of disaffection was so rife in the back country that "the Common Language of the People is, that they would full as live, be under the French as the English Govt."[40] This language has remarkable resonance with the reports of Carteret's agent more than forty years earlier. These attitudes had no official status, but the violent eruptiveness of the Massachusetts General Court over the sloop question, and soon afterward over the much more serious issue of parliamentary taxation, does suggest that the leadership had some affinity of mind with those whom they led.

The organization of the empire, if it can be dignified by such a word, left many vacant and ill-defined spaces. Into these spaces, Parliament was inching its way. But there was very little sign before the conclusion of the Seven Years' War that anyone in Parliament had worked out a general theory of the scale and sweep to be announced in 1766. Where that was being done, it was by obscure civil servants whose views were made known only to a few ministers. The Board of Trade's own more ambitious designs had been frustrated by Walpole's neglect in the early 1720s. Parliamentary sovereignty was being gradually developed, amplified bit by bit, from parliamentary action. But the colonies in turn only gradually became aware that they had anything to fear from this source, because they had assimilated the Glorious Revolution to their own cause and had acquired an early habit of looking on Parliament as either inactive or benign.

CHAPTER THREE

The Challenge of Parliament

When Americans attributed parliamentary powers to their own assemblies—and this is the most familiar of all the themes of assembly politics in the eighteenth century—they were thinking exclusively of the House of Commons. But they were involved in a complicated form of mythmaking. The House of Commons they had in mind belonged only to a limited and very uncharacteristic phase of the seventeenth century; it was the heroic House of Pym and Hampden, defying a tyrannical monarch in the name of liberty, property, and the Puritan religion; it was the House that went on in later years to raise armies that defeated the king and gave rise to the rule of Cromwell. At this point the record grew more obscure. Cromwell's parliaments, as they grew less and less representative and exerted ever less power to control the executive, became a less conspicuous model of either religious or republican virtue.

Nevertheless, the same forces represented the true spirit of English national and religious life. This view of history had the advantage of taking out all element of surprise. When these forces rose up to overthrow James II, they were behaving in a manner true to their nature and consistent with what the colonists expected of them. About the murky complexities of English history the colonists had little information and less curiosity, for the very good reason that the information they possessed already answered the only questions worth asking and did so in very satisfactory ways. In a sense they were pitting the myth of the seventeenth century against the reality of the eighteenth and then transferring the qualities of the mythological seventeenth century to their own assemblies. It can hardly be surprising that the misunderstanding that developed between them and the British authorities sometimes struck the latter as having overtones of sedition.

We can no longer take seriously this view of the growth of the power of Parliament as a development immanent in the parliaments of Elizabeth, rising out of the natural progress of the wisdom and wealth of the English people under the Stuarts, to reach its full flower only after a few brief and unwarranted interruptions by Charles I and James II. It did not wait to be unfurled by Whig hands from the Revolution Settlement; as I have already suggested, it was not even foreseeable in 1689 (which is by no means to deny that there were Whigs who hoped for it). It seems timely, therefore, to look more closely at the historical development of English government in the long aftermath of the Glorious Revolution and to relate this history to the government of England's colonies.

The conventional phrase "the Revolution Settlement," which I have just used, would have been a misnomer in 1689. William's acceptance of the throne implied no specific settlement, nor was the later pattern of constitutional relationships even beginning to be clear. There is a difference between a "balanced constitution" and a "limited monarchy," and it is significant that the idea of "balance," although first advanced by Charles I as an ingenious tactical maneuver, caught on much later with the consolidation of Whig power in the eighteenth century. England under William and Mary was emphatically and primarily a monarchy. As late as 1710 one of the managers of the impeachment trial of Dr. Sacheverell, for uttering a species of alleged Tory sedition, was satisfied to describe the "nature of our constitution" as that of "a limited monarchy."[1] Richard Cumberland, one of the authors of the ideas of benevolence which did much to transform the deity in the eighteenth century, was content to call England a "regulated monarchy." This was a Whig expression from the Exclusion crisis.[2] "Cato" later described England as a limited monarchy in which "the Laws are known, fixed and established." The constituents of the government, the ministry, and all subordinate magistrates had their own certain, known, and limited spheres.[3] The reception of Newtonian celestial mechanics had given political scientists a new and highly satisfying metaphor, which assimilated politics to the fixed and regular laws of the natural order.

This terminology, however, was far from describing any such concept as parliamentary government. William had to summon a parliament every year because he was engaged in a costly war with France; the need to commit England's resources against France was his chief reason for consenting to cross the Channel in the first place. Only after strenuous objections did he agree to the Triennial Act of 1694; and that act was as much an indication of English distrust of a foreign monarch as of any determination that the country should be ruled through Parliament rather than by the king's ministers.

It cost many English political leaders great anguish to discard the authority conferred by divine right monarchy. The Convention Parliament revealed this painful reluctance; and even when, years later, leading members of Parliament were claiming the right to make the king's ministers accountable to Parliament for actions taken in the king's name, as an instrument of intervention, none of them wanted to use Parliament's financial power in the prerogative areas of war or diplomacy.[4] The choice of his own ministers was another branch of the king's undoubted prerogative; for Parliament to take a hand in that process would have been just as upsetting to the uncertain "balance" of the constitution as an overexertion of executive power would have appeared—and did appear—to later generations.

In the difficult, strife-torn years between William's accession and the death of Anne, the country came to be governed by a variety of institutions, or of persons holding institutional positions. The Bank of England—surely deserving to be called such an agency—was created in 1694 by the Whigs by an act of Parliament. But the Board of Trade, created in 1696, was a counterblow by the crown. It was a manifestation of the king's determination to keep the large and increasing areas of trade, navigation, and the colonies firmly under royal control; appointments were made by the crown, free from any responsibility to Parliament. William saw the board as a potential check on parliamentary power, and Bishop Gilbert Burnet remarked at the time that the debate on the subject was a clear issue of prerogative power.[5] The board's weaknesses have been explored by historians and were only too well known to its members. Its activities were confined to collecting information and making recommendations; it was inferior to the Privy Council, and it lacked executive power. It was also subject to the recurring weakness caused by lightweight political appointments. Yet the board had the most direct bearing on colonial affairs of any agency of the British government. It was the Board of Trade which in the early 1700s strongly advocated that the proprietary colony charters should be called in and placed under royal control; it was the board which gathered all official information about colonial economic development, investigated erosions of the navigation laws, and in 1721 drew up a comprehensive proposal for colonial reorganization, to take place under its own aegis. That plan would have made the Board of Trade the supreme executive authority over the colonies.[6] Its failure, or default at the hands of Walpole's administration, represents a silent turning point of which the colonies were unaware.

Another development of the reign of William III was the

practice by which the king's ministers met to discuss royal policy and, when required, to make decisions. These meetings were undoubtedly promoted in part by the king's absences abroad, but they also took place in his presence at home. We need not here go into the details of the development of the cabinet council; we do need to recognize that its growing power resulted from the associated process which assigned collective responsibility to the crown's ministers. By the end of Anne's reign, this idea of cabinet responsibility had begun to gather weight as a recognized institution. Once the cabinet considered itself responsible to Parliament as well as to the monarch, and once Parliament held it to that position, the monarch's freedom to act through individual ministers was beginning to be restricted. The colonial governments developed no counterpart. The governor's council, unlike the cabinet, was itself a legislative upper house as well as an appeal court; its members had no departmental responsibilities and no individual executive duties. Colonial governors had to learn the art of working with the leading members or factions in the assembly and could seldom be neglectful of assembly politics; but no member of the executive branch held an assembly seat. It is customary to attribute the weakness of the colonial executive to its want of effective patronage, a condition that improved, from the governor's point of view, with the mid-century wars. But the lack of an executive presence in the legislature was a departure from English constitutional practice which represented a chronic weakness; it passed unnoticed, partly perhaps because it was built into the governmental structure, but also because current constitutional theory regarded the presence of the executive in the legislature as an abuse, a form of corruption. Country interests in Britain periodically introduced "place" bills in an ineffective attempt to restrict Treasury influence in the House of Commons. From this point of view, the colonies could congratulate themselves on being purer practitioners of country ideology than the British. Meanwhile, the council had many important functions, but it was not a house of lords. For all these reasons, the colonial constitutional structure imbued the representative branch with opportunities and powers that tended to impair the operational effectiveness of the idea of balance.

In England the Privy Council still wielded considerable influence as the monarch's adviser on peace and war, and after the dissolution of Parliament, when it lost power in face of the cabinet, it remained the executive authority in colonial affairs—and colonial affairs were increasing in national importance. It might even be argued that colonial assemblies were often more aware of the Privy Council than were ordinary members of Parliament in Britain.

Between them, the individuals holding office under the crown and in the complex of bodies primarily of royal appointment ran both the government of the country and the administration of the colonies. But certain functions fell to Parliament and to Parliament alone. Only a parliament could raise the taxes needed for William's and Anne's long wars or for those that broke out after 1739; only a parliament could pass such legislation as the Acts of Trade and Navigation. It was in Parliament that individual ministers could be called to account, the extreme case being the medieval procedure of impeachment. England, moreover, was a country divided by party animosities of intense bitterness, which did not altogether disappear under Walpole's oligarchy. To get the crown's business through Parliament, the managers or "undertakers" found it increasingly necessary to rely on organized support among the heterogeneous membership who controlled the purse—a privilege jealously reserved by the Commons. And the more they planned and calculated to arrange this support, the more fully the House of Commons entered into the ordinary operation of the political system. In these ways there developed a complex, unplanned, but increasingly normal connection between the running of government business and the meeting of parliaments.

I put that central noun in its plural form. For it was not yet clear that the English constitution contained the single, permanent entity known, in our terminology, simply as *Parliament*. Whenever the monarch needed a parliament, writs were issued, elections held, and the Lords and Commons of England duly assembled at their sovereign's command. But after the Parliament had been in due course dissolved, there was no parliament, there were no members of parliament. Between sessions of parliament, all the executive bodies I have mentioned continued in existence and could in many cases have done very well without its assistance.

As early as July 1689, William admitted to Halifax that as long as there was war he would always want a parliament— and that "so long they would never be in good humour."[7] The implication is inescapable that, like Charles II, he would do without parliament whenever he could. The normal Whig view during the Convention debates limited uncustomary assertions of parliamentary power to emergencies; there seems to have been little or no anticipation of a general increase in the role of parliaments in government.[8] The emergence of Parliament as a singular noun and as the great, governing power of the realm was gradual, uncertain, unpredicted, and unpredictable. In reviewing the period down to the mid-eighteenth century, P. G. M. Dickson, in his magisterial study of national finance, concludes that Parliament "became a real focus for the major interests within the country," but "at the beginning of the period this seemed unlikely to happen." He even remarks that it seemed more likely that Parliament would go the way of the Polish diet. In the light of this judgment, his summary of Walpole's achievement gains special force; for by the time of his fall in 1741, Walpole "had firmly established . . . the supremacy of Parliament in the formulation and expression of national opinion." He had also established the need for a leading minister to sit in the Commons, for the careful management of both court and Parliament, and for the leading role of the Treasury in the executive government.[9]

But even in the reign of Queen Anne, it would not have been apparent that the increasing authority of Parliament would accrue to the House of Commons; it was the Lords who appeared to be gaining in governmental power.[10]

Many generations of historians have been brought up on a gradual but decisive process in colonial history known as "the rise of the assembly." If there are certain qualifications to be made to this general view, they relate principally to the fact that the New England assemblies began their lives with such considerable powers that they could hardly have risen much further. After losing them under the Dominion, Massachusetts regained many of them in an aggressive burst of legislation during the first few years of the new charter.[11] Historical distance may foreshorten the past, but it does not reveal a linear process. But after the imposition of a new and more restrictive charter, Massachusetts had some ground to regain. In Virginia, which was ruled by its council without either governor or assembly for the years 1706 to 1710, it would have been a bold man who would have predicted the powers assemblies acquired in the course of the eighteenth century. By gradual accretions, won by fighting on specific issues whenever the occasion arose, assemblies gained powers with which in most cases they had not begun—or which they had subsequently lost.[12]

The direction of the argument is now, I hope, becoming clear. The rise of the colonial assembly to the full extent of its claim to parliamentary powers, and the rise of Parliament itself, were developments taking place through approximately the same period. Moreover, although Parliament raised itself to great power as the highest of constitutional authorities, as "sovereign" when conjoined with the monarch, its actual claims to participate in government remained surprisingly limited. Parliament, of course, raised supplies. It passed both public and private legislation. In the eighteenth century the distinction was emerging, but no preference was given to what we

now call government business.[13] Parliament also aired grievances and debated large public issues. But Parliament did not
govern; the ministry, and increasingly the crown agencies, did
that. What Parliament could do was to call a ministry to account. In 1741 Sir Robert Walpole was no longer able to control the system he had done so much to create, and he fell
from power, not as a result of being dismissed by his sovereign but after an adverse vote in the House of Commons.

Turning to look at all this in colonial perspective, it becomes
a little easier to appreciate the nature of the difficulties experienced by the colonies in coming to terms with Parliament.
And these difficulties were morally and psychologically compounded by the colonial habit of honoring Parliament as the
instrument of national liberation from popish tyranny. They
gave it historic credit for its role in defeating the tyranny of
Charles I and credit again for saving both the nation and the
colonies from James II. With the passage of time, but only
gradually, Parliament confronted the colonies in a new guise,
as the instrument of Britain's mercantile classes, of the government's interest in national wealth, in its need for naval
supplies, and in its broad responsibility for protecting and
extending a mercantile empire. In these ambitions the colonies had an ever-increasingly important part to play; but that
part nevertheless reflected their subordination to the aims and
purposes of Great Britain.

The ambiguity of the colonial attitude toward Parliament as
late as the 1730s was revealed in the course of a dispute between the Massachusetts General Court and Lieutenant Governor Dummer. The assembly had insisted on approving all
accounts before permitting the treasurer to make payments
of public funds on the governor's warranty (as required by
the charter). To stop this interference by the House, the crown
sent the governor an additional instruction. Instructions were
commands from the crown to subordinate officers of the executive, a procedure in which the colonial legislature had no

right to interfere. Yet both Council and House of Representatives twice petitioned to have it withdrawn and then in 1733 actually appealed to the House of Commons to intercede with the king. Not surprisingly, the House rejected the appeal as "frivolous and groundless, an high insult upon his Majesty's government, and tending to shake off the dependency of the said colony upon this kingdom."[14] The remarkable part of this episode is not the reaction of the Commons but the temerity of the Massachusetts legislators. If they had succeeded they would have set a possible precedent for parliamentary interference in matters of government; but they took the risk, partly because they had reason to hope that the administration would not proceed, but also in the mistaken belief that the British House of Commons was in some residual sense "on their side" in a dispute with the executive.

British aims and purposes were manifested in the ever-increasing range and complexity of the Acts of Trade and Navigation and in the more direct interventionism in the acts restraining colonial manufactures. Yet it remained true that British governments showed very little inclination or intention to govern the colonies. There is no evidence of a desire to develop a detailed administrative control; and even if that desire had existed, the machinery did not and would have taken substantial resources to develop.[15] This is what the British government began to do through the medium of parliamentary legislation after 1763. Before that time, even appeals from colonial governors for support against recalcitrant assemblies received sympathy rather than effective action. Both the Duke of Portland as governor of Jamaica and Burnet as governor of Massachusetts at different times felt let down by the home government, in Portland's case after a very severe denunciation of his assembly's "inexcusable, and intolerable behaviour."[16]

Power and authority thus issued primarily from the crown. For longer than the first half of the eighteenth century, Parliament felt its way gradually and tentatively toward colonial administration, manifested no general desire to involve itself in the government of the colonies, and persistently declined even to back up executive power by its own legislative authority.[17] The corollary of this argument, as we have seen, is that the colonies themselves had not got used to any general theory of parliamentary authority, and their own view of government had no place for a British Parliament to play an interventionist role in their affairs. But an argument on the lines I am suggesting must now face a formidable obstacle. In 1740 the Massachusetts legislature established a land bank to create a new supply of credit for the province's sorely distressed economy. A highly influential minority, mainly of overseas merchants, regarded this policy as a prescription for economic disaster. Outvoted at home, the minority appealed to Parliament, which responded with an act to repeal the Land Bank Act of the provincial legislature.[18]

This was by no means the first British intervention in colonial financial affairs. The power to mint coin was reserved to the royal prerogative and was never extended to the colonies. The power to issue paper money was somewhat more ambiguous and in any case proved extremely difficult to control. In the 1720s, when South Carolina was moving toward resumption by the crown, its currency affairs were a center of constant controversy. In 1722 the provincial Commons House passed a bill for the issue of a new paper currency that was met with a royal veto in response to an appeal to the Board of Trade from elements in Charleston's merchant community.[19] The recent collapse of the South Sea Company had sent a shock through British trading and financial circles whose waves hardened into a permanent distrust of paper currencies that was reflected in generations of subsequent policy. Since colonial opinion itself was divided, and the overseas merchants, whose contacts with Britain were the most intimate, were hostile, it is hardly surprising that Parliament was later influenced to intervene on their appeal from Massachusetts.

The form taken by British intervention in South Carolina had been a royal veto. The repeal of the Massachusetts Land Bank was an undoubted act of parliamentary intervention. But over this episode a new difficulty confronts the theory that the colonies were not accustomed to and in principle did not believe in the legitimacy of such an exercise of parliamentary power, taking positive form in the contrary opinion of Thomas Hutchinson. In his own account of the incident, which took place shortly after his first entry into legislative politics, Hutchinson explains that the authority of Parliament to control all public and private persons and proceedings in the colonies was, in that day, questioned by nobody.[20]

This is a sweeping assertion. But the chief justice, lieutenant governor and later governor, and leading contemporary historian of Massachusetts speaks of the history of his own province with an authority that cannot be lightly brushed aside. His opinion raises at the highest level the question of the real state of colonial opinion in general and that of Massachusetts in particular about the nature and extent of parliamentary power in the colonies.

Debate about the land bank passed very quickly from questions of economic morality to questions concerning the wisdom and propriety of referring provincial matters to the mother country. Writers to the Boston papers took both sides. One expressed anxiety about any appeal to England affecting charter privileges; another replied that charter privileges did not include the liberty to make paper money without restraint.[21] In this latter view, the paramount need was for an act of Parliament to protect those who owned any property. At the beginning of the controversy, William Douglass wrote a pamphlet on colonial currency questions which clearly—if tendentiously—identified the issues in terms of domestic political parties. Playing on an ancient theme in Whig—and colonial—demonology, he described the compulsory acceptance of paper money in payment for debts as "Despotick and arbitrary Government." Since the representatives were generally free-holders, many of whom were in debt, there was no justice to be had from the provincial legislature, an argument that led straight to Parliament. These grievances "call aloud, for some speedy and effectual relief from the Supreme Legislature the *Parliament of Great Britain*."[22] He later noted with satisfaction that Parliament seemed likely to abridge the privilege assumed by the plantations of issuing their own bills at rates imposed by their own will. There was no question here of any doubt: Parliament was the "supreme and absolute law-giver."[23]

These views plainly reflected the merchant minority's defenses and linked their interests with British power. The argument suited the occasion. But it would henceforth be difficult to deny that in certain circumstances Parliament could intervene. The force of this argument may well have contributed to the difficulties later experienced when Massachusetts spokesmen had to define themselves in relation to parliamentary taxation. Hutchinson himself was a member of the same circles, and it is altogether possible that he did not move where he would have encountered serious opposition views.

Opposition views nevertheless existed and were widespread. The defiant attitude of the assembly in 1741 drew from the recently installed Governor William Shirley a warning that it was an error to suppose that the charter conferred the privilege of striking bills of public credit to pass in lieu of money, and his speech gave rise to a long and heated debate. Eventually, the House so far ignored the governor's warning as to pass a new act for the emission of £40,000. Technically, this had a different basis, being associated with the support of the government, but it was little less than defiance of royal authority.[24] Shirley certainly thought so, for he at length felt obliged to dissolve the assembly for defying both king and Parliament.

The best contemporary account of these events, evidently

written from close experience, appeared in the form of a pamphlet in 1744. The author records that the House of 1741 made as its first choice of Speaker a member whom the governor felt obliged to negative; at which they chose Mr. Fairfield, a man characterized for his "general Opposition for Government," who had "openly in his Discourse bid Defiance to the Act of Parliament then lately pass'd for the Suppression of the Land Bank scheme, and was a Person, whom the House would not have chosen for Speaker at any other Time."[25] The governor soon afterward dissolved the intractable House.

Open opposition in the House of Representatives was compounded by the continued circulation of land bank notes in the countryside. Shirley had some difficulty in persuading the directors and partners of the company voluntarily to obey the act of Parliament; the vote to disband was "difficultly obtained, and carried only by a bare Majority, many of the Partners being warmly of opinion to stand out in defiance of the Act of Parliament."[26] Before the end of 1740 the council had already begun to dismiss justices of the peace (including Samuel Adams, Sr.) who had been parties to the scheme, and these dismissals continued into 1741 as certain justices appear to have defied the government.[27] A year later Shirley still found it necessary to enforce the law by proclamation.[28]

This evidence makes it impossible to sustain Hutchinson's opinion, which must be regarded as historically one-sided. His political stake in this retrospective view of public opinion in Massachusetts was, of course, irreversible. From the standpoint of a holder of high office in the administration in face of the antiparliamentary outcry after 1764, it was important to be able to demonstrate that all the recent opposition to parliamentary powers was based on a new theory which had no previous place in the history of Massachusetts. Hutchinson had not seen the private opinion of Lord Loudoun, who as commander-in-chief encountered some genuine back-country attitudes. In 1756 Loudoun had noted that "it is not uncommon for the People of this Country to say, they would be glad to see any Man that dared exert a British Act of Parliament here."[29] This was consistent not only with other observations he had made, which have been quoted, but with the long stream of subterranean opposition of which we have seen eruptive signs at intervals since the overthrow of Andros.

In 1757 Loudoun accused the Massachusetts Assembly of questioning the authority of Parliament in connection with a quartering act for soldiers serving in the province. Hutchinson, then lieutenant governor, wrote a message denying this charge, which the assembly adopted as its own. Hutchinson comments that the legislators' denial might have been influenced by the consideration that they now hoped for reimbursement from Parliament for their wartime expenditures—but he emphasizes that it represented their real convictions.[30] Even at this late date, Hutchinson was asserting that the province was governed by men whose loyalty was unquestioned and whose acceptance of the theory of sovereignty withstood the test of local resentments. Yet nothing of deep constitutional significance (except the Writs of Assistance case, which in no way touched on Parliament) had happened in the interval when, five years later, in the dispute over the commissioning of the sloop, James Otis virtually excluded Parliament from his discussion of power in Massachusetts.[31]

This was not a view that Otis himself was to sustain with great consistency. But in its time it was significant. Undoubtedly, after the fall of Fort Duquesne and Quebec, all of the colonies, and especially New England, felt safer than at any time in twenty years. But the war was still on, and its ultimate terms of settlement were unknown; no one could be sure that Britain would seize Canada from France. The struggles over the Revenue Act and the revolt against the Stamp Act lay in an unforeseen future; no one can describe the sloop episode as yet another "beginning" of the Revolution. Yet here at this date, Otis calls the assembly "the great council of this province, as the British parliament is of the kingdom," a clear assumption of parliamentary title.[32] By making these claims for the assembly, he excluded those of Parliament. By relying heavily on Locke, whom he linked with William III and with the Convention Parliament of 1689, he drew the principles which give authority to government away from Parliament and into the assembly in its representative capacity.

Long years of political laissez-faire had served the colonies well. Under the tradition of "salutary neglect" they prospered and their populations grew rapidly. By mid-century close observers were calculating that their population had doubled in just over twenty years, a remarkably accurate estimate.[33] Although economic development brought its own problems to the different colonies with an increase in urban poverty, new pressures on land, stresses felt within the family, and the first experiences of soil exhaustion in the tobacco lands, not to mention socially divisive religious upheavals, there prevailed a widespread faith in the future. The future lay in the land and the sea—the latter both a vast resource of productive wealth and the great avenue of commerce for a rising economy. The wars in which the great empires of Europe clashed with each other also brought the colonists' needs and interests into closer proximity and interdependence with their home country. Friction was occasionally inevitable, and occasionally it was serious. But colonial Britons had little cause to complain of the general system of which they formed so valuable a part and still less cause to expect anything better.

The peculiar nature of this colonial relationship was recognized by a British administrator, James Abercromby, who brought personal experience as an elected representative in South Carolina, and subsequently as an agent for North Carolina and Virginia, to bear on his recommendations for reform of the system. Writing privately for the information of the Board of Trade, he struck two notes which do not seem entirely consistent. On one hand, he saw that acts of trade would have to be amended in great detail and the system brought under much tighter regulation; and these reforms would require acts of Parliament. On the other, he recognized that there was something peculiar about Britain's colonies: "From their first Establishment they stand upon a kind of Independency in Government." And again, although they are subjects, "they are subjects under peculiar Circumstances, formed into separate Societys, that in time they may feel their new Strength."[34] Abercromby did not get very far in his expressed aim of making the "natural" and the "political" ties between the colonies and the mother country coincide.[35] But his general tenor supports the thrust of the argument that parliamentary intervention was rare. His references to precedents for such intervention, which were required to justify his proposals, revealed a recognition that such acts had been called forth only to remedy specific errors or to alter general conditions. He went further than many contemporaries would appear to have gone when he claimed for Parliament the power to alter charters; but he did not suggest an intention to govern the colonies through Parliament, which would have been a very different—and difficult—procedure.[36] In a second tract, written in 1774, he expressly stated that "on extraordinary occasions only" had Parliament, with the king and the Privy Council, interfered "in the Regulations of Colony Government."[37] This meant alterations of frames of government, not the regulation of policy. Both views recognized a considerable area for colonial autonomy.

Parliamentary authority had a more easily recognized role in intercolonial matters on which the colonies could not act for themselves. It was not out of keeping with a considerable measure of internal legislative autonomy that the Albany conference of 1754 recommended that Parliament should pass an

act for the proposed colonial union—though only after ratification by the peoples of the colonies. Benjamin Franklin
himself believed the union would need an act of Parliament.
Within a few years the war in America brought British forces
into the colonies on an unprecedented scale and gave rise to
bitter disputes about quartering; but the English Mutiny and
Quartering Act of 1689, which still operated in Britain, was
not held to extend to the colonies. This gap was not filled by
Parliament until 1765. In the presence of an imperative demand for billets for British troops on service in the cause of
the colonies, the assemblies of Massachusetts and Pennsylvania stepped into the vacant area with measures of their own,
which the Earl of Loudoun held to be inadequate. But from
the present point of view, the interest lies in the fact that colonial legislatures saw significant areas for the extension of
their own authority on their own soil. It comes as no surprise,
then, that the parliamentary act of 1765 met such widespread
colonial resentment and resistance: here was a real clash, on
the ground, between the two sets of legislative authorities.[38]
New York, which had not passed its own measure, also re-
sisted and succeeded in defending its citizens' homes.

Massachusetts challenged the intervention of Parliament
when it passed the Revenue (or Sugar) Act of 1764 but failed
to make it into a general colonial issue.[39] Parliament very
promptly provided another opportunity next year with the
Stamp Act. This act of internal taxation touched a constitutional question of exceptional historical and ideological salience; it also managed to affect nearly all the classes (not
including specifically only the clergy) who were best placed
to express their opposition and to mobilize resistance. But we
can now see that the reaction did not spring from unfertile
soil. The exact relationship of Parliament to colonial government, as distinct from the general field of imperial regulation,
had never been clearly defined. Parliament had reimbursed
Massachusetts for its share of the heavy expenses of the col-

onies in the French and Indian War; and nobody seems to have complained that there was anything unconstitutional about that. The great advantage of the system as a going concern rather than an object lesson in political theory was that for practical purposes it did not need to be too clearly defined. The process of definition depended as much on experience as on theory. During and after the war, experience tested the vague outlines of theory and found them wanting.

As early in the great controversy as the summer of 1765, Americans began to discuss the view that their connection with Great Britain was confined solely to that of subjects of the crown. "I could wish," said a writer in *The Providence Gazette*, "that some *civilian* [i.e., civil lawyer] would settle how far the *people of America* are dependent on the *people of Britain*: I know of no *dependence* or relation, only that we are common subjects of the same king."[40] After the Townshend tariffs had renewed the turmoil, William Hicks of Philadelphia published a series of newspaper essays inquiring into parliamentary power which aroused so much interest that they were soon reprinted in book form in New York. "Every distinct colony," he said, "has hitherto been considered as a particular plantation of the crown," and he added that they were very badly governed at that.[41] Benjamin Prescott, who composed a series of fair-minded and dispassionate essays in the form of letters, beginning in 1768 but not published until 1774, observed that the Parliament of England or Great Britain was nowhere mentioned in the charters. "The King and Privy Council may negative our laws, but there is not a word intimating that Parliament have anything to do in the Matter" or that it was vested with any powers to make laws for the colonies. Nor could he find any covenant or agreement by which the colonists had subjected themselves to the laws of Parliament.[42]

Prescott later turned to consider Governor Francis Bernard's argument that the powers of Parliament were coextensive with those of the crown. This was a dangerous threat to the integrity of the colonial defense; if it were found to be good British constitutional law, the colonial attempt to distinguish between crown and Parliament would be blunted. The fundamental colonial answer was historical; such coextensive parliamentary power had grown with the growth of Parliament but had not been implicit in the original position when the colonies were founded; it followed that the colonies were not obliged to consent to developments in the interpretation of the constitution about which they had never been consulted. Prescott developed this line of reply by referring once again to the charter, which expressly gave the General Court the grant to make laws. The term used was a grant of "full" powers, to which the governor, in controversy with the House of Representatives, had replied that "full" powers did not amount to "sole" powers. As Prescott remarked, it was up to the governor to explain the distinction.[43] As early as 1768 Prescott had concluded that the king reigned *separately* over Great Britain and the colonies and that no coextensive parliamentary power existed. James Wilson reached essentially the same conclusion in 1770, but like Prescott published his view after the outbreak of renewed controversy in 1774.[44] Thomas Jefferson traveled the same way to reach these conclusions in his *Summary View of the Rights of British America*, first written as the draft of instructions to the Virginia delegates in the Continental Congress and subsequently published as a pamphlet.[45]

If Americans were questioning whether Parliament had the right to intervene, they were unwillingly forced to admit that it had the power. The New York Assembly fought a series of tough battles to avert actual suspension by Parliament for its refusal to implement the Quartering Act of 1765, compromising its popularity if not its principles by granting large sums of money for the support of British troops.[46] Each colonial struggle had the effect of narrowing the ground on which an

American assembly could take its stand; but the deeper effect was to increase the danger that Americans would seek shelter on different ground, whether or not it was covered by the British constitution.

Parliament was no longer succeeding in making the colonies happy. In the course of the argument, British spokesmen and theorists had to rely heavily on the principle of indivisible sovereignty. The appearance in 1765 of Blackstone's *Commentaries on the Laws of England*, a book which almost immediately acquired authoritative status and was accepted as such in the colonies, could only have the effect of defining the choice. No theory existed under which the colonies could be held equals to the mother country, and none could be devised in time to resolve the crisis. Blackstone hardened feelings and narrowed the choices by his definition of law as that of the will of a superior over an inferior.[47] Meanwhile, the British backed their magisterial view of sovereignty with emotions of outraged paternalism. Only in 1778–79 did another British colonial administrator, William Knox, who, like Abercromby, had had colonial experience, suggest that America should be given constitutional protections along with the assertion of parliamentary power.[48]

By this time Lord North's rather unconvincing gestures of conciliation had also failed to conciliate, because the American leadership, carrying with it a considerable section of public opinion, had decided to locate sovereignty on American soil. There is no reason to suppose that they realized that they were involved in a process that would lead to a redefinition of sovereignty.[49]

The Scottish-born lawyer James Wilson, who was making his career at the Philadelphia bar, brought the threads of our argument together in his well-known pamphlet published in 1774, *Considerations on the Nature and Extent of the Legislative Authority of the British Parliament*. This argument would have been unintelligible in 1660, and, if intelligible, barely defensible in 1689. By 1774 it had become acceptable and would soon be considered obvious. Since no one had any right by nature to authority over any other, said Wilson, all lawful government was founded on consent: "The consequence is, that the happiness of the society is the *first* law of every government." A question followed: "Will it ensure and increase the happiness of the American colonies, that the parliament of Great Britain should possess a supreme, irresistible, uncontrolled authority over them? Is such an authority consistent with their liberty? Have they any security that it will be employed only for their good? Such a security is absolutely necessary. Parliaments are not infallible: they are not always just."[50] Wilson in no way challenged Blackstone's "superior will" theory of law or the indivisibility of sovereignty; his challenge was directed at Great Britain's claim to exercise these powers where they could not serve the first law of government. And this led him to the conclusion that the superiority of Great Britain over the colonies was to be rejected.[51]

The crisis thus brings us back to our former conclusion. The historic sense of community had collapsed, and it had collapsed under the test of utility. The language of the law and the constitution has led generations to conclude that the revolutionary crisis was ultimately a crisis over sovereignty, but this is correct only to the extent that questions of constitutional definition can be considered "ultimate"! The truth that gave life and urgency to the argument was that it was also a crisis about *legitimacy*. The legitimacy of the institutions of government was coming more and more to be valued in the light of their effectiveness in representing the multiplying interests of the community; in short, in promoting their happiness.

CHAPTER FOUR

The Problem
of Communication

E very new phase of the history of both Parliament and the colonial assemblies has revealed them as subject to the pressures of change. It is not altogether surprising that the direction should have proved to be similar in Britain and in Britain's colonies, since in the widest sense they were all parts of the British nation. One of the irreversible consequences by which change could be identified was the gradual recognition that the performance of government and, in extreme crises, its very existence were subject to utilitarian criteria. During half a century beginning in 1640, the English nation confronted two such crises, from which the colonies were bound to draw their own lessons. These lessons were part of the experience on which the colonial leaders drew when it fell to them to try to interpret the meaning of Britain's policies toward them in the following century.

Colonial assemblies had from their beginnings been sensitive to local opinion and justified their existences by their ability to respond to the demands and pressures of those formations which came increasingly to be called "interests." The English House of Commons preferred higher ground. At different times it had different ways of describing itself and, in the process, of defining its functions. It had hardly ceased to be the High Court of Parliament when it became "the great inquest of the nation." More specifically, it represented one of the great estates of the realm, leaving the care of others— ecclesiastical and civil—to the House of Lords. The actual business of the Commons during the eighteenth century re- flected the House as coming increasingly to be an arena in which varieties of interests exerted their several pressures, often taking the form of private bills for local purposes, but also transforming themselves into the policy of the govern- ment of the day. Whereas merchants had an interest in the advantages conferred by the acts of trade, and manufacturers gained by restraints on colonial production, the government saw the gain in terms of national wealth and its concomitant naval and military strength. Only very gradually, however, and with marked reluctance, did the House of Commons come to recognize its effective functions as including the represen- tation of interests, a pragmatic description that had about it less glamour and less dignity than that of the estate of the commons of Britain.[1]

To perform these functions required a practical and system- atic rapport with the people of the shires and boroughs who were directly or indirectly represented in Parliament through the electoral system. To put it more theoretically, when Parlia- ment, and especially the House of Commons, claimed to be the rightful source of authority on the grounds of its repre- sentative character, it assumed an obligation to fulfill that character. If members of Parliament were to know the minds of their constituents, to reflect them faithfully, and to retain their confidence, some theory of communication between them became a requirement of the role of the representatives.

This view of the matter, however, is easier to state from the standpoint of what we expect of modern democracy than it would have been at any time in the history of the first British Empire. To live in Britain or the United States or any other of the representative democracies that take their model from these sources is to be reminded (if we did not already take it for granted) that we have an indisputable right to know what goes on in our legislatures. The system of government requires a steady flow of information between the people and their representatives; it would be virtually impossible to construct a theory of democracy which did not include this as a vital element. This free flow of information—a two-way flow, from constituents to their representatives and from the legislature to the people—is a logical extension of the principles of pure democracy. If there is any need of an official theory of public access to legislatures, that is not because they are democratic bodies but because they are *representative* bodies. We have come to assume that political representation derives its justification from the belief that it is the most efficient means of legislating according to the precepts of democratic theory. This requires that representatives should be accountable; and we cannot hold our representatives accountable unless we know what they are saying and how they are voting.

That sounds obvious enough. But clear, linear reasoning, which appears to us as a requirement of constitutional logic, has never been a necessity of history. Representative institutions are capable of existing, and for centuries did exist, not only without support from the theory as I have expressed it but in positive defiance of it. In the last analysis it would be illogical to divorce representation from accountability, and I am not suggesting that English or American constitutionalism has ever countenanced an absolute divorce. But the historic truth is that the colonial assemblies of the first British Empire developed as contemporaries of a parliamentary system in Britain; that both these systems claimed to be representative but at the same time rejected all ideas of democracy and recognized no obligation to provide public information about debates or divisions in the legislature. Only the *outcome* of legislative proceedings, in the form of laws and resolutions passed, and in certain cases summaries of proceedings were made known to the public. There is a very great difference between informing the public of an outcome and letting them know how it was reached.

The transition from that view of legislative responsibility to the more modern view, which regards public access and legislative visibility as matters of principle, is historically recent. It dates, broadly, from the 1760s to the 1790s; its formal development, particularly in literary terms, occurred somewhat earlier in Britain than in America; but when it occurred in America the rationale was more clearly defined.

Representative institutions have had good historical reasons to be aware of their own vulnerability. They have at different times been threatened with intimidation of individual members, collective violence, purges imposed by soldiers, and corruption both by private interests and by the executive. All of these constituted threats to their independence and therefore to their freedom to act according to their own judgment and conscience. The first source of danger in England was the crown. In face of the threats of Charles I, the House of Commons advanced from 1641 to 1642 its own claim to represent the people; and with moderate consistency and varying degrees of plausibility it has made that claim ever since. There may, therefore, seem to be an element of paradox in saying that the second source of danger to the independence of the legislature was seen to be in the people themselves—or at least in hostile elements, which led to the same results.

The events of the early 1640s broke on a Parliament which had a long tradition of stubborn defense, and advance, of its own privileges. The House of Commons first established the privileged status of its members' utterances in 1512.[2] Throughout the Tudor reigns the business of the House was always held to be profoundly confidential. With Queen Elizabeth's secretaries of state sitting in the chamber, it can hardly be supposed that members felt very well protected against royal disfavor, and we know that they were not. But the House of Commons commanded respect; its doings were not fit for prattle, and it was not considered right that members should be in any way subjected to the pressure of local or interested opinion. Writing from his experience of the Parliament of 1571, in which he sat for Exeter, John Vowell, giving himself the name Hooker (which had an Exeter connection, though I do not know if that was his reason), mentioned that the clerk of Parliament was to keep its records and added, "The councel of the house he may not disclose." This order was strictly enjoined on members: "Also every person of the Parlement ought to keep secret and not disclose the secrets and things spoke and doon in the Parlement house, to any manner of person unless he be one of the same house: upon pain to be sequestered out of the house, or otherwise punished, as by order of the house shall be appointed."[3] No nonmember was to be allowed to enter during a sitting. Hooker laid emphasis on the reverence due to Parliament, and it is possible to catch the feeling that its dignity would be impaired by the comings and goings of strangers and by out-of-doors gossip. The queen herself conveyed the same impression very plainly in 1585 when she rebuked members, telling them "that she heard how parliament matters was the common table-talk at ordinaries, which was a thing against the dignity of the House." Four years later, the Speaker responded to a request from a member by telling the House "that speeches be not any of them made or used as table talk" and reminded them that they were "the Common Council of the Realm."[4] This remark gives us a clue to the principle which ordained secrecy. At a session dealing with business affecting private parties the House would sometimes admit outside parties who had a cause to plead; as with the Privy Council, members' own deliberations were confidential. But members' private interest in these rules was made clear by Sir Edward Hobby in 1589, when he complained of a false report made to "a great personage" of a speech of his in the House; and he thought this had been done since "Mr. Speaker his late admonition generally given to this whole House against uttering of the secrets of this House either in table-talk or Notes in Writing." His resentment was understandable because he had been sharply rebuked by some "great personage (being no Member of this House) for speeches delivered Friday last."[5] Members may often have broken these rules, but none would have been likely to challenge the need for them.

Yet there is an element of paradox which cannot be altogether dismissed. Private bills affected the fortunes of their promoters, and when these questions involved giving preferences to one interest rather than another, it became difficult to separate private interest from public policy. In 1584–85 three groups of artisans, the tanners, the curriers, and the shoemakers, all had bills before the House of Commons, and their members had a natural interest in what was said in the House, of which they evidently heard rumors. John Bland, a currier, complained openly that "the curriers could have no justice in this House" and asserted that the shoemakers' bill was passed when only about fifty members were present and when the curriers' friends in the House were absent. He also complained that the tanners' bill had not been properly read, some leaves of it having been left out of the reading. For these remarks, Bland was called to the bar of the House. He got off, Sir John Neale observes, "with taking the Oath of Supremacy, making a humble submission, and paying his fee to the Serjeant." But a fee of twenty shillings "was no small sum for a poor craftsman." The tension between parliamentary privacy and public interest became much more acute with the monopolies controversy toward the end of the reign. Sir Robert Cecil revealed more than he intended when he warned the Commons in 1601 "that whatsoever is subject to a public exposition, cannot be good. Why! Parliament matters are ordinarily talked of in the streets. I have myself heard, being in my coach, these words spoken aloud: 'God prosper those that

further the overthrow of these monopolies. God send the prerogative touch not our liberty!' "[6] Provocative words, indeed;
and it is difficult to believe that their speaker was ignorant of
the identity of the occupant of the coach within earshot.

From time to time the House discovered a stranger in its
midst. Such persons were always examined; one such apprehended in 1580 explained that he did not know the orders
and was discharged after "willingly taking the oath against
the Pope's supremacy." In 1593 another, who proved to be "a
simple, ignorant old man," was pardoned and discharged on
making his humble submission and paying the serjeant's fee.[7]
The fear of papist spies undoubtedly played its part in this
anxiety, but the enforcement of the Oath of Supremacy was a
formal act of penitence. It is unlikely, for example, that anyone would have attributed the currier John Bland's outburst
to religious disaffection, but he also was required to take
the oath.

The liberties of the House of Commons were protected by
its privileges. It was between 1586 and 1604, after hearings
on contraverted elections, that the House established its own
authority over the credentials of persons returned as members.[8] The rule of secrecy was also a matter of privilege, capable of being enforced by the House on members as well as
outsiders. American colonial assemblies adopted and enforced the same rule, if anything more assiduously than the
English Commons.

The Commons were willing to take a more relaxed view on
certain occasions. There seems to have been no breach of
privilege when speeches of particular eloquence were reprinted in literary collections. There are, moreover, early instances in which the journals themselves reproduced speeches
delivered in the House. In 1580 the Commons had a quarrel
with the queen because they had ordered a day of fasting and
prayer, which she considered part of her prerogative. Three
speeches, including two by the vice chamberlain and the

chancellor of the exchequer, were recorded in the journals.[9] In 1606 the issue of immigration touched off a debate which also found its way into the journal. The debate was begun by an unexpected tirade against the Scots from Sir Christopher Piggott, Kt., from Buckinghamshire, who found an excuse to rise and "entered into by-Matter of Invective against the Scotts and the Scottish Nation, using many Words of Scandal and Obloquy, ill-beseeming such an Audience, not pertinent to the Matter in hand, and very unseasonable for the Time and Occasion, as after was conceived." Mr. Fuller, anticipating the principles of Enoch Powell, attacked the practice of general naturalization for the Scots. "God hath made People apt for every Country," he said, "some for a cold, some for a hot Climate, and the several Countries he hath fitted for their several Natures and Qualities." There was an obvious danger of being flooded: "Look in the Universities; there many of our own, very worthy, not preferred," and he warned the House, "It shall not be good to mingle two Swarms of Bees under one Hive, upon a Sudden." The debate that followed was reported in snatches, but Sir Francis Bacon's reply occupies nearly a column.[10]

This recording of speeches was an exceptional event. It began no practice and is difficult to explain. But we may infer that feelings ran very high and that Fuller and other opponents of the free admission of the Scots felt strongly enough to want their opinions to appear in the record—even if it was seldom read by nonmembers of Parliament. It was to be a general though not an invariable rule that speeches and divisions were entered in the journal when members had an interest in recording their opposition. The first division of which a numerical report appears took place as early as 1554. There was another numbered division in 1558 on a question of privilege and another in 1563 on the election of Richard Onslowe as Speaker. These were rare events, and it seems significant that the next to occur, in 1571, was on bills which made certain offenses treasonable; after "many long Arguments," the two bills were joined together into one and engrossed, "with the Difference of 36 Voices."[11]

Sir Robert Cecil's warning of 1601 reveals clearly that privy councillors had no desire to open the deliberations of Parliament to out-of-doors opinion. But a nascent conflict is hinted at here, which suggests a flaw in the doctrine of privacy itself. Had not the impertinent voice overheard near his coach cried out, "God send the prerogative touch not our liberty!"? If it ever became the business of Parliament, and particularly of the House of Commons, to protect the liberties of the people against the royal prerogative, then privacy would be placed under very great stress because the Commons would need the support of the people.

In view of the seriousness of the conflicts between the early Stuarts and their parliaments, it must be considered a tribute to the strength of the doctrine that its practice was so firmly maintained. But by protecting its privacy, the House of Commons was beginning to make use of its procedures as a defense against undue pressure from the crown. It is noteworthy that the issue of religion showed no sign of abatement when strangers were apprehended within doors. In April 1628, during the debate on the king's supply, according to the record, "one stood almost an hour in the entry, called Philip Parsons, a Scholar, lately come from beyond the Seas: who called to the Bar, and, professing himself of our true Religion, sent out." The committee deputed to examine him reported favorably the next day: he was "a scholar of Oxford, always of good reputation for learning and religion." He had taken the oaths of allegiance and supremacy both before leaving England and on his return. He had begun studies as a doctor of physic at Padua. The House discharged him on payment of the usual fees. A few days later another man, standing in the doorway, was called to the bar, confessed he was present through ignorance of the rules, and was pardoned on the strength of good testimony to his religion and character.[12]

These incidents, in themselves trivial, remind us that the

House was attentive to its own privacy, in its own interests, which it enforced as a matter of privilege through its own procedure. Yet this privacy could not indefinitely remain a private matter. In Charles I's reign the principle was no longer being enjoined on the House of Commons by privy councillors anxious to preserve the king's business from public discussion. In no previous reign had any parliament experienced more urgent need to protect its privileges and liberties *against* the royal prerogative. In May 1628, the Commons debated the Petition of Right, a remonstrance to the king against incursions into the rights and liberties of the people.[13] From the point of view of publicity, the most remarkable aspect of the House of Commons procedure in this tense and dangerous conflict was that it never published the petition or in any way communicated it to the people. As representatives of the people, the members of Parliament were repositories of a trust; but that trust did not call for appeals to public opinion. It could most faithfully be discharged within the formalities of the relationship between the Commons and the crown; if the House of Commons was on the way to winning the initiative in this relationship, to use Wallace Notestein's famous phrase,[14] it was doing so within existing rules of procedure. This was, perhaps, a fatal mistake, if made with the highest intentions. When Charles dissolved Parliament and embarked on his long period of arbitrary government, he could do so without risking the opposition in the countryside that might have arisen if the Commons had armed themselves in advance by proclaiming themselves defenders of the people's liberties. The next eleven years' experience would go a long way to erode this confidence in the ancient conventions. On the next occasion, the mistake was not to be repeated.

After convening the new Parliament in 1640, Charles I brought home to the Commons as never before the importance of protecting their privacy against the crown. As the crisis deepened, after the opening of a new Parliament in 1641, the need became more acute and reached physical form when, in January 1642, the king invaded the House in search of the Five Members. But the doctrine of privacy contained certain difficulties for a body whose entire right to exist was based on its claim to represent the people. The difficulties were implicit in the equally powerful and far more popular practice of instruction.

When corporations sent members to a parliament they habitually assumed a right to instruct them as to the course to be pursued for the advancement of local interests. The practice was already regarded as normal in 1571, when a member argued in the Commons that instructions should be confined to local matters because no instructions could "give even the wisest man a full sense of the place for which he served."[15] Knights of the shire were also made aware of local opinion, though they seem to have been less subject to specific instructions than the burgesses. Only very rarely before 1640 did the local people step beyond the bounds of their parochial interests to instruct their representatives on matters of general policy, although signs of this wider perspective made occasional appearances in earlier parliaments.[16] Beginning in 1640, and gathering force in 1641, constituencies—as we would now call them—began to urge their representatives to venture into fields of general policy; and it was from this point that Derek Hirst has noted that public opinion for the first time became a major political factor. He also reports that in 1640 the town of Cheddar, in Somerset, spent four pence on a book of parliamentary proceedings; and that petitions of the counties and of peers demanding a new parliament were circulating in various parts of the country by the late summer of 1640.[17]

In theory, the right of instruction cuts clean across the principle of parliamentary privacy. The electors can know whether their instructions have been obeyed only if their member makes a candid report to them of what has passed in Parliament. At least until the conflict began in 1641 to evoke divided loyalties in both country and Parliament, however, this contradiction raised no difficulties. The story of the session would normally be told only when members got home, and their reports to their electors could have no effects on day-to-day proceedings. It is doubtful whether any theoretician of the system would have denied that the people had a legitimate claim to hear from their own representative a report of proceedings which bore directly on their own interests; and when wider issues, such as royal demands for subsidies, touched their persons or purses, it seems equally likely that they would have expected to hear from their representative a justification of his votes. Since parliaments normally met infrequently and only for a few months at a time, this contradiction between instruction and privacy appears more theoretical than real. But the stable conditions in which the shires and boroughs of England could confine their expressions of concern to the repair of decaying harbors, the improvement of roads, and the advancement of local trade were coming to an end. Government under Laud and Strafford had already reached deep into the communities, and when Parliament met it was natural that the communities should expect more of their government. The crisis dividing the king from many members of the House of Commons very soon developed into a conflict among the people themselves. Both sides understood the importance of public opinion, and wherever Charles traveled in the country he took a printing press with him.[18] But the House of Commons did not broaden its appeal to the people until it had first tried to make fast its defenses against the king.

In 1640 there existed no order against the printing of reports of parliamentary events, presumably because it had never yet occurred to anyone to try. The House of Commons very early decided to bring this situation under its own control, however, and in February 1640, it took the first step toward setting up a committee for the licensing of printed books.[19] In November, orders were given to keep strangers out of the chamber.[20] Events now moved in two directions. The licensing procedure was soon turned into a regular censorship, further advanced by several ordinances passed in 1641 and 1642.[21] These included strict rules that papers issuing by order of the House were to be printed only under the Speaker's hand, an arrangement that had about it the advantages of a closed shop for the official printer. These rules were steadily elaborated. In 1647 both houses passed an ordinance against "unlicensed or scandalous pamphlets," suppressing all unlicensed publications, including reports of parliamentary proceedings, and setting up licensing procedures.[22] This anticipated the Licensing Act of 1662, by which the restored monarchy succeeded to and enlarged the powers of its predecessor by instituting a formal English censorship.[23] The most important point for the relationship with the public was the control by the House of Commons of all information about its own proceedings. Many infractions occurred in the next century and more, but this principle remained at the base of the claim to parliamentary privilege over publication until the entire system began to collapse in 1771.

Censorship was made necessary by the other direction of events, however, which was exactly opposite. On 17 March 1641 John Pym made a two-hour speech in the House of which an abbreviated version, taken from members' notes, was printed and distributed as a pamphlet; and this, according to a contemporary, was the first occasion on which a speech made in Parliament was published to the world at large. The effect was at once to increase the size of the political public by increasing its awareness of the House of Commons, while engaging it in the Commons' cause against the crown.[24] Very soon a flood of such material spread through the country, with fairly substantial reports of debates and resolutions.[25] These gradually died out in 1643, no doubt under the weight of parliamentary censorship, but not before they had given the people of England an unprecedented opportunity to form political opinions on the basis of news from Parliament—opinions which in principle could have had electoral consequences, if new elections had been in prospect. But in the circumstances of the times, the consequences were more likely to be military than political.

The conflict between crown and Parliament led directly to a constitutionally vital development in the relationship between the House of Commons and the people. In 1642 Henry Parker, the first and most forcible theorist of parliamentary sovereignty, argued that Parliament's power was arbitrary because the authority of the people was irreversibly entrusted to it. No power existed by which it could be controlled.[26] During 1641 it had already become necessary for the Commons majority to assert a virtual identification between the elective branch and the people, a claim itself based on the assumption that had now to be made that "the people" constituted the nation.

But this view required another assumption—that the House of Commons was a united body. This was a historically justifiable standpoint; it had long been the custom that after a vote, the whole House symbolically agreed to the bill on which it had just divided.[27] A modern commentator has carried the point further by arguing that the majority held that Parliament could not function with an avowed rift; this was the significance of the refusal to permit publication of the views of the minority after the close vote on the Grand Remonstrance. William Chillingworth was sent to the Tower in December 1641 for "Reporting wee had sides and parts in the howse which was but one bodie, soe to sett a division amongst us."[28]

Unfortunately, however, "sides and parts" did exist among members of the House of Commons, and Chillingworth's report must have struck the majority as a threat to their position, which may help to explain their vindictiveness. The country can hardly have doubted the existence of the divisions when reading the widely distributed accounts of debates. The vote on the Grand Remonstrance, taken after a debate lasting from noon on 23 November 1641 to two o'clock the following morning, was carried by 159 to 148. This was immediately followed by another long and hotly contested debate on whether it should be addressed to the people. After an adjournment, this topic was resumed on 15 December, when the decision to publish was taken by 135 to 83.[29] By this time, symbolic unity could have highly practical implications, whose effects were hard to distinguish from repression; and the mood of the majority was further indicated by the trial of Strafford, which produced the first exercise in parliamentary history of the coercive use of publicity about members' votes in the chamber. The names of fifty-nine M.P.s who had voted against Strafford's attainder were posted up on the Royal Exchange under the title, "The names of those men, who to save a Traytor, would betray their Country."[30] It is hardly surprising that attendance in Parliament began to fall. Yet this retributive mood was not gaining universal support, and the first historian of this Parliament, writing as early as 1647, noted that much disaffection was already found among the common people in the summer of 1641.[31]

Although the army council was obviously not designed as a representative institution of government, it behaved in some ways like a constitutional or parliamentary convention when it debated the fundamentals of government in December 1648. The record of the Putney Debates is of unusual, if incidental, interest for the history of such events because the clerk, William Clarke, took notes of speeches and votes. These notes, whose scribbled congestion itself tells something of the atmosphere of the discussions, report a remarkably democratic encounter between soldiers of all ranks. There is no sign that common soldiers were intimidated by officers; on the whole, the lower ranks voted with some consistency against their seniors. Not having been made public, these records carry perhaps little general significance for the history of representation, but they stand as an authentic document of a moment of peculiar intensity in England's constitutional history.[32]

When legislatures revealed their proceedings by any form of official publication, they almost always did so as a claim on the people's support against the executive and by strong implication advanced the theoretical claim that the representative ingredient of the government was the one that gave legitimacy to a complex or multipart system. That process reached a culmination in the American colonies when the elected assemblies, superseded by the provincial conventions, successfully established their claim to represent the popular party among the people, which is why the previous chapter reached the conclusion that the crisis, defined in constitutional terms as being about sovereignty, was really a crisis over legitimacy.

The need to make this claim presented legislative bodies with particular difficulties when they were deeply divided, as was the House of Commons in 1641 and as colonial assemblies were to be at certain points in their controversies with British governors. In the crisis over the Grand Remonstrance, both majority and minority sought public support for their conduct in Parliament. In the debate on whether to print the dissent of the minority, speakers for that proposal pointed to the tradition of the House of Lords. The peers had long been entitled to declare their dissents in their journals. To this, Sir Simonds D'Ewes logically replied that "the non-usage of this for soe many yeares of this manner of Protestation in this howse when ther weere soe many occasions for it, and some great matters carried by a pluralitie of a few votes only, doth stronglie evince that it ought not to be used in this howse, and the rather because it hath been constantlie used in the Lords howse."[33] The peculiarity of the position of the Lords was, of course, that they were not representatives. Each peer sat in his own right. It might well have been argued that the representative character of the Commons gave them just as good a claim to publish their dissents. But this view was not compatible with the fiction of the unity of the House, to which the Lords had never subscribed.

The doctrine that the elected branch represented the people—coupled as it came to be with the idea that election conferred legitimacy—merged with another convention of parliamentary political thought. This was what we may call the "whole nation" view of representation. On this view, each elected member had a duty to consider the interest of the whole nation as superior to his own or to that of his constituents. The "whole nation" conflicted with the primacy of special interests, and, as Burke found much later in his famous dispute with the electors of Bristol, it could not be reconciled with the doctrine of instruction.[34] Instruction continued on special occasions, but the "whole nation" view came closer to being accepted on most sides, whether court or country, as standard constitutional theory. It appeared in as many words in the country paper, *The Freeholders Journal*, in 1721 in language almost identical to that made famous by Burke half a century later. In between these dates, the Earl of Egmont, a country peer who among his other interests was a Georgia trustee, wrote a scathing attack on "Tory faction" in which he denounced certain instructions drawn up by misguided inhabitants of Westminster with a view to distracting members of Parliament from their public duties. "These being published in the printed papers, were, with Diligence and Expedition sent into the Country as the Sense of this great Metropolis, to be thence taken for the Voice of the whole people of *England*. . . . [T]hey published a Pamphlet, to convince them, that it was the duty of every member of Parliament, to vote in every instance as his Constituents should direct him in the House of Commons—a Thing in the highest Degree absurd, for *it is the constant and allowed Principle of our Constitution that no Man, after he is chosen, is to consider himself as a member for any particular Place, but as a Representative for the whole Nation.*"[35]

The "whole nation" view had to overcome the resistance of

the primacy of local agency, and the tension can be glimpsed at a moment of crisis in the debate about printing the Grand Remonstrance. One member raised the question, in the case when two members from a single county disagreed, and by inference involved their electors in their disagreement, which of them should be said to represent the constituency?[36] While members "involved" their constituents they could hardly be detaching themselves to achieve the perspective of the whole nation.

To carry its message to the people, the House of Commons had to inform them of its actions. The practice of publishing the *Votes* of the House—meaning decisions taken each day, not divisions—began early in the Long Parliament and continued intermittently. The Commons forbade publication after 1665, when Charles II's secretaries of state began to publish *The London Gazette*, and this restraint almost certainly reflected renewed tension with the crown.[37] Andrew Marvell, in his voluminous letters to his constituents at Hull, frequently reported divisions with numbers voting on either side, and no one took him to task for that; but these were addressed specifically to his own electorate and would hardly have been considered a breach of privilege; on the contrary, they reflected the legitimate intimacy of a member with his own people.[38] The official publishing of *Votes* was resumed in 1680 but remained sporadic through the years of crisis. In a debate on the question of printing the *Votes* as late as 1689, several members expressed fears about letting the Lords and the crown know what had passed in the Commons, and on one occasion the Commons ordered a book to be burned, apparently for no other reason than that it contained reports of parliamentary proceedings. Sir Richard Temple, speaking in the debate of 1689, balanced the matter by recalling the Oxford Parliament and objected to "commissions that Gentlemen had from their country about the Exclusion-Bill." He hoped that "we shall not imitate Holland, to go to our principals for

Instructions."[39] Early in 1689 the House of Commons refused to permit publication of its *Votes*, but later the same year, with the tribulations of life under the Stuarts behind them, the Commons once again decided to publish them, after which the practice became permanent. They were made up at the end of each day's proceedings and usually published the next morning; the *Journal*, on the other hand, was a fair copy composed from day-to-day notes but written up at the end of the session or at long intervals; the *Votes* are therefore sometimes a more reliable guide to events.[40]

The tight official control of parliamentary news was fully compatible with continued restrictions on information about what passsd in Parliament. In 1694 the Commons clamped down on a source that had recently become popular—the reports appearing in the London newsletters, made up from information supplied by the clerks of the House (who earned a supplementary income from the printers).[41] The official *Votes* continued to circulate widely, and with the advantage of parliamentary franking, they kept people in the country informed of the business of Parliament—often the only way of finding out about intended measures that might affect their livelihood. The demand was vigorous, and in the 1730s the *Votes* sold about two thousand copies a day, usually at two pence each.[42] This circulation seems to have declined only when the newspapers began to report parliamentary debates in the late 1760s.

There was a close connection between the development of public interest in political life, whether because it affected great national policies or because of local interests, and the use of parliamentary information for direct political purposes. As early as 1660 a leaflet calling itself "The Grand Memorandum, or a True and Perfect Catalogue of the Secluded Members of the House of Commons, sitting 16th March, 1659" was published "to prevent mistakes, and that the people of this Nation may see and know who have been their Oppressors, and the fatal

Betrayers of their Liberties, by erecting High Courts of Justice, and acting many other enormities, etc., And that they may be the better guided in their FUTURE ELECTIONS." This was a tactic similar to the posting of the names of Strafford's supporters some twenty years earlier; but on this occasion it heralded the arrival of the specific intention of influencing voters at elections. In 1681 a Whig tract warned electors against M.P.s of known Roman Catholic proclivities; in 1690 the Whigs circulated a list of 150 Tories who had voted against recognizing the abdication of James II, and the Tories replied by circulating a list of members who had voted for the Corporation Bill, whom they described as "Republicans, Fanatics, Latitudinarians, or Atheists."[43]

The intense party warfare that was already several years old and continued until the installation of George I was a novel phenomenon, which brought equally profound changes in constitutional practice. Parliament, and specifically the House of Commons, gradually became both the forum and the fulcrum of national politics. The government of Britain could be influenced, perhaps even changed, through the representative branch and even through electoral changes in a comparatively small sector of that branch. Geoffrey Holmes tells us that between 1702 and 1715 there were 113 "weathervane" seats out of 513 in the House, involving 69 constituencies.[44] In many of these, only one seat was at risk, the other safe. Since this amounted to the entire area through which electoral influence could be exerted, these seats were all the more important and the struggle to win elections the more intense.

This makes it easier to understand why the "whole nation" view took such a firm grip. The issues were now by general consent national issues. And the party struggles for control of the executive converted parliaments into a forum for debating the issues, which in turn provided an agency for assisting the executive in decisions, with fatal effects if the executive could not command the confidence of Parliament. It would be incorrect to say that at this date parties had become part of the constitution; but the government of the country could and did operate through a sort of agency of parties, which in turn accepted the legitimacy of parliamentary decisions.

The House of Commons did not record division lists—a practice which had to wait until 1834.[45] Members could, however, make up their own lists for political use, either in the management of the House or in the constituencies. There has been a small but intense concentration of interest in these division lists in recent years, but as some of their students have pointed out, it will not do to place too much stress on their importance.[46] For one thing, their numbers are not sufficient to give dense or continuous information. Romney Sedgwick lists about twenty for the period 1715 to 1754; but some of these were printed in several places where it was thought they might have influence, while some were made public in sensitive constituencies.[47] A further difficulty is a result of the practical circumstances in which they were made up. No officer of the House of Commons was responsible for keeping a record of how members voted but only of the numbers on each side. A member bent on making a list had to write his notes as members filed into the chamber from the lobby; and when it is remembered that divisions were often taken by candlelight and that most members wore wigs, the risks of error become painfully obvious. Many of these lists must undoubtedly have been completed by subsequent consultations or from inference.

There can be no doubt about the seriousness of the exercise, however. After a debate in the Commons on the Treaty of Utrecht in 1713, in which a clause offering commercial reciprocity to France was defeated by 196 to 187, a handbill was put out to publicize the division list with the obvious intention of damaging the electoral interest of the minority.[48] The general election of 1722 excited particular activity because it gave the first opportunity for an electoral protest against the Septennial Act of 1716. *The Freeholders Journal* called for the identification of members who had voted for "several obnoxious measures" and advised electors to examine their candidates. It added the sound country sentiment that men with large properties were the fittest guardians of the liberty of their nation.[49] At least two lists were published while the elections were in progress, with the aim of digging out late voters.[50] Some ten years later, *The Craftsman* reported the printing of false lists to mislead the public on the Excise Bill of 1733.[51] When the Place Bill was reintroduced in 1739, Lord Chesterfield observed with weary sarcasm that afterward, "it will be necessary to print the names of those who voted for or against it; and then fresh instruction from every county or borough both in England and Scotland."[52] By the 1770s, however, lists were printed for their general news interest and no longer for party political purposes.[53]

All this activity was unofficial. None of it represented any relenting of the official secrecy surrounding the debates and proceedings; and this in turn gave an air of unreliability to some of the reports. The Jacobite printer Nathaniel Mist complained that he sometimes had great difficulty in getting into the chamber, even though he paid out substantial sums in fees to the clerks;[54] the possibility of false information was presumably made worse by the fact that it could not be corrected from official records. But none of this tended toward a more open policy. The House of Commons was, moreover, the sole guardian of the nation's finances, but that was a power it kept to itself and never offered to share with the people.

This point makes a striking example of the observation with which I began. No one would have denied the representative principle on which the House of Commons was based, and few at this date would deny its representative character. But representation did not mean communication with the electors, and only on the septennial occasions of a general election did it mean accountability to them. Even then the opportunity afforded was of a very limited character, and the tendency of Walpole's administration was to limit it still further. Supply bills were never printed; Walpole had no desire to stimulate out-of-doors discussion of his government. He even refused to allow the printing of the Excise Bill in 1733— and then complained that the public outcry arose from ignorance of its provisions![55]

Since parties not only appealed to public opinion but in a very strong sense created it and enlarged the politically conscious public, it is not surprising that these activities stimulated interest in what was going on within Parliament. Notwithstanding the formal prohibition, in 1711 Abel Boyer announced his intention of reporting debates in his journal, *The Political State of Great Britain*, which continued to do so until 1737. Not until 1731 did *The Gentleman's Magazine* offer to compete; stimulated by the success of the example, *The London Magazine* entered the field in 1732. These latter two began by simply pirating the reports in *The Political State* but soon took to printing their own versions. These magazines took advantage of a loophole in the order against reporting, which made it possible to publish reports after the close of the session.

This gap was closed by the House of Commons in 1738. The proceedings were introduced by the Speaker, who drew attention to the breach of privilege. Some of the members who spoke on the subject expressed formal concern about the liberty of the press but assured themselves that this was not the issue; and the main objection raised was to the extreme inaccuracy of many of the reports. Walpole, who concluded the debate, attacked the reports for the false impression they gave to the country and remarked that the magazine reports sometimes made the vote of the House come down on the opposite side to the weight of the argument as presented, all of which tended to make the House contemptible. It was clear that he was dissatisfied with the reporting of the administration.

The debate was not without its humorous moment, when Pulteney observed that a member sitting near him, meaning Walpole himself, had once offended in precisely the way now complained of, by writing a pamphlet which reported the proceedings of the Parliament of 1713—and no succeeding Parliament had taken this amiss. To this Walpole replied that the Parliament of 1713 was an exception. It had contained members who were willing to set aside the succession then impending to the throne. And even so, he and the printer had been aware that they were running a risk.[56]

No member opposed the motion, which was unanimously carried. And it gave rise to no outcry in the press. A note in the *Parliamentary History* attributes this silence to preoccupation with the threat of war with Spain.[57] But it was a strange silence from a press whose freedom was impaired, leaving one to wonder whether parliamentary reporting was not regarded more as a form of entertainment than a political right.

The press was not entirely muzzled, however. To evade the suppression, the two London magazines resorted to the device of reporting the debates of "Magna Lilliputia" or "a political club" or the Roman senate. The names of speakers were transparently disguised. Samuel Johnson, though he never set foot in the House, was the most celebrated of these retrospective speechwriters, applying his ample eloquence to skimpy notes. It was in this connection that he once remarked that he saved appearances tolerably well, "but I took care that Whig Dogs should not have the best of it."[58] Johnson once experienced difficulty containing himself during a dinner at which one of the guests extolled the extraordinary power of a recent speech by Pitt. "That speech," Johnson at last broke out, "I wrote in a garret in Exeter Street."[59]

This practice of recording debates was difficult to keep up.

It placed a great strain on the magazines' resources and on the concentration of the reporters; even public interest seems to have declined in the later 1740s, and parliamentary reporting was discontinued, not to revive until the 1760s, when it was a direct result of intense competition among the London newspapers. The printer John Almon believed that the future of the field belonged to the magazines and that it would be beyond the powers of the newspapers to keep up the pace.[60] Parliamentary repression may thus actually have sustained the efforts of the printers. The rival papers claimed to have the most authentic reports, and they lost circulation when their news was inadequate.

The situation was complex as well as increasingly tense. Politicians had come to appreciate the importance of a good press and wanted to control it for their own ends—which no politician, least of all the administration, could do. But many of the reports caused offense, as did the printers' manifest disregard for the dignity of Parliament. Since every report constituted a breach of privilege, a clash was bound to come. It came in the well-known events of 1771, when Colonel George Onslow complained of a misrepresentation in one of the papers, which replied with an insult that could only have been intended to provoke the wrath of the House. Onslow had contrasted present practice with that of Sir Robert Walpole's time, when, despite the most violent opposition, transactions were published only after the close of the session "and then only in a decent manner." He asked that either the offenders be severely punished or the standing order be revised. Members on the other side admitted that abuses took place but asserted that ministerial speakers were foremost in abusing gentlemen who differed from them. They argued that prosecutions would only provoke the sales of libels, not put a stop to them.[61]

The minority did not fail to argue for the constitutional rights of the public. According to the report, they added that "the practice of letting the constituents know the parliamentary behaviour of their representatives, was founded on the truest principles of the constitution, who even ought to know the particular votes they gave in every case, as the constituents had no other powers over their representatives, when once chosen, but to determine whether they were proper to be re-elected."[62] Burke maintained the same view, as he had done in his recent *Thoughts on the Causes of the Present Discontents*, in which he urged the use of "frequent and correct lists of voters in all important questions."[63]

The House summoned the offending printers to appear at the bar, where three of them apologized. When the fourth, John Miller of *The Evening Post*, defied the House, it sent its messenger to arrest him. To do this the messenger had to enter the precincts of the City of London, a medieval corporation with its own jurisdiction. A constable who was on hand at once arrested the messenger for assault. There followed a hearing before the lord mayor of London, Brass Crosby, and two aldermen, one of them being John Wilkes, who ruled that Miller's arrest was illegal but allowed the House of Commons messenger bail.[64]

The great cause of press freedom now turned on the privileges of the corporation against the authority of the Parliament of Great Britain. The House committed the lord mayor and Alderman Oliver to the Tower, where they remained, but only until the end of the session in May 1771—about two months. Wilkes, however, was prudently left alone.[65]

The policy of the North administration was not founded on mere inertia nor on an outmoded conception of parliamentary dignity. There were certain occasions, particularly relating to American affairs, when the administration considered that the national interest would not be served by the diffusion of information. After the affair of the printers, the administration, left with a victory enfeebled by the knowledge that offending printers could play the same trick again, nevertheless did not give up either the principle or the practice. In April 1777, Temple Luttrell raised constitutional objections to the exclusion of strangers, and the following year, Charles Fox urged that the public had a right to know what its representatives did in Parliament. In this he was joined, not for the first time, by Burke.[66] Such was Lord North's preoccupation with secrecy that Parliament was not told of the conditions of the Howes' mission to the colonies in 1776, and Henry Conway moved unsuccessfully for an address to the king to inform the House.[67] But gradually the administration gave up the struggle, or rather, enforced the principle of privacy with decreasing frequency. The gallery could still be cleared of strangers on the motion of a single member, which would of course remove the reporters as well as members of the public; but between 1780 and 1834 this seems to have been done only twenty-one times.[68]

The conditions for reporters were inhospitable. They frequently had to tip the clerks in order to get into the House. Some of the reporters were content to pick up Westminster gossip. But the ones who conscientiously strove to give accurate reports found that they could not keep up with the pace of speech and resorted to omissions and constructions. In 1783 James Perry, editor of *The Daily Gazetteer*, instituted a system of team reporting which introduced a higher standard of reliability.[69] It was also Perry's policy to give impartial reports, which must have gone some way to reconcile those members who had not unreasonably objected to the reporting of debates on the ground that the reports as printed were frequently inaccurate and often deliberately distorted. The history of parliamentary privacy in the eighteenth century, when Parliament had nothing to fear from the crown, has to be read in the light of the fact that most reporting was to a greater or lesser extent opposition reporting.

The public gradually came to rely on its parliamentary news service, and administrations found they could live with the press. In 1803 Speaker Abbot marked a quiet transition that had taken place in official attitudes by allowing reporters to occupy a fixed part of the gallery.[70]

This question of access to the galleries raises the more general problem of the right of members of the public to overhear debates. We have seen the Commons interrogating persons who had in all apparent innocence strayed into the doorway in the 1620s. In 1640 and again in 1641 the Commons had every reason to preserve the confidentiality of their proceedings from royal knowledge, at least until the House resolved to make its position known. The problem kept coming back. Thus on 5 March 1662, "Upon information that several persons, not Members, had come by the back door into the Speaker's chamber whilst the House was sitting; it is ordered that the back-door be constantly kept shut, whilst the House is sitting."[71] In 1688 the Commons ordered their sergeant-at-arms to arrest strangers, and in 1705 this order was extended to meetings of committees of the House and was thenceforth repeated at the beginning of every session.[72]

This rule was seldom treated with great respect. Members no doubt often wanted their families or friends to be present, and members of the public felt a legitimate interest in their rulers' proceedings, so that attempts to enforce the order periodically enlivened the parliamentary spectacle. John Hatsell, the recorder of parliamentary procedure for this period, states that whenever any member called the Speaker's attention to the presence of strangers in the gallery, the Speaker had instantly to order the sergeant to execute the rules of the House. But he adds, "It very seldom happens that this can be done without a violent struggle from some quarter of the House, that strangers may remain: Members often move for the order to be read, endeavour to explain it, and debate upon it, and the House as often runs into great heats upon this subject."[73] Strangers were not often excluded. In the Parliament of 1768, whose procedural record is well documented, they were kept out on twenty of more than six hundred days on which the Commons sat.[74] But on the other hand, it must be remembered that exclusion could be a matter of policy, with more serious implications when the issues were important. The most politically significant example of selective exclusion was the administration's policy of holding all the debates of 1774 on American affairs in private. The purpose was probably to avoid disclosing differences of opinion and particularly pro-American speeches which might have encouraged colonial resistance.[75]

One of the features of the rising public interest in the slightly more urbane political scene under the Whig oligarchy was an interest in Parliament on the part of the female sex. On one occasion in 1743, two ladies sitting in the gallery urinated through the floorboards onto the members below. One member had a new suit spoiled, and another, no doubt glancing up at the source of this unexpected cascade, was nearly blinded.[76] Women nevertheless continued to attend, until in 1778 an order to clear the galleries gave great offense to many ladies present. Thereafter it seems that they were allowed only to sit in a ceiling compartment from which they looked down vertiginously on the men who ruled their lives. They were readmitted to the galleries in 1834.[77]

Events crowded on Parliament in the eighteenth century, and so did the many and growing number of interests in the country. These interests cumulatively swelled a public interest. After the emergence of the competitive newspaper press, and in the turbulence created by the troublesome issues of the later 1760s, parliamentary privacy was a slowly losing cause—increasingly undermined by the members of Parliament, who themselves wanted to report their speeches to the public. Parliaments and administrations gradually discovered that it was easier to work with the public than in seclusion from it. In the process, Parliament became much more fully integrated into the life of the nation. It learned to listen as it had not done since the death of Queen Anne. If another half century was to elapse before it succumbed to Reform, this was in no small part because, by better communication with the people, the House of Commons went some of the way to reforming itself.

CHAPTER FIVE

Telling the
American People

American assemblies did not begin their lives with the aid of formal guides to parliamentary procedure. The practice of keeping their own records was a business necessity they discovered for themselves; but it was also one which in several cases was required of them by the agents of royal government. These requirements brought assembly journals into existence long before there was any need to convert the manuscript into print and long before it had entered into the heads of either branch of government that the common people might have a legitimate interest in or right of access to the records of their rulers' proceedings.

Once journals existed, however, the proceedings they recorded could at any moment acquire political significance. This point came into focus when assemblies started to quarrel with the crown or its agents. The royal commission which visited Virginia to investigate the province in the aftermath of Bacon's Rebellion subpoenaed the assembly's records. Robert Beverley, the clerk, refused to hand them over, got into a violent controversy, and persuaded the House of Burgesses to record a formal protest against this "Violation of their Privileges." So convinced were the burgesses that the right to privacy was a genuine parliamentary privilege and that they as a provincial legislature were entitled to such privileges that they took the extraordinary step of sending a remonstrance to the king. Such presumption was soon proved unwise. Charles II took personal offense and ordered the Privy Council to prepare a code for Virginia; Beverley was removed from office and held under arrest for a year. When in May 1680 Lord Culpeper arrived as royal governor he carried instructions commanding the clerks of both houses to submit their journals, and also the laws passed, for royal review. Official English interest was now on the increase; the Privy Council also demanded a sight of the journals of Jamaica's House of Representatives and reports from all the councils and secretaries of royal provinces.[1] Governors were also expected to transmit a great deal of information in their correspondence, which remained a major source for British governments throughout the colonial period. Much later, in 1759, we find Governor Horatio Sharpe of Maryland observing that he always sends Lord Calvert, the proprietor, a copy of the journal of the lower house as soon as the work of copying can be completed.[2]

Six years after Bacon's Rebellion, a bitter quarrel over tobacco planting divided the burgesses of Virginia from Governor Sir Henry Chicheley. The legislators now discovered political advantage in taking a step toward the people and took home copies of their journal to read to their constituents at public meetings.[3] It is unlikely that these copies were printed; members of the House probably read aloud from handwritten copies of the manuscript. The move was tactical; it implied no recognition that their electors had a general right to know. More commonly, it was far closer to the self-protective instincts of assemblymen to maintain their collective privacy against any hint of scrutiny from any direction. In 1682, two gentlemen were rebuked by the House of Burgesses for the offense of letting a vote of the House be known outside. A printer called Bruckner was required to post a bond for the very large sum of £100 for unlicensed printing of the laws of the colony—a breach of the assembly prerogative of appointing its own printer; two years later Captain John Purvis was summoned to appear for publishing a book of laws without license, "to the Great Scandall and Contempt of the Gouernment of this his majesty's dominion."[4]

On occasions when the House took a vote—in parliamentary language, "divided"—the clerk had the choice of either confining himself to noting the outcome, affirmative or negative, or of recording the votes cast on either side. But with one exception, the listing of the names of members voting was unknown in the seventeenth century. The exception was provided by Maryland, where in the session of 1637–38 the assembly decided that all freemen were members of the assembly. In 1637 a resolution was recorded as "Passed by all the Freemen," and in 1640 the negative voters were listed in a division.[5] Absentees were allowed to vote by proxy. This, however, cannot be considered strict precedent for the recording of divisions; the assembly was too literally an assembly for that; it was not so much a representative body as a communal meeting. By 1640 a representative assembly met in Maryland.[6] The practice of recording lists continued into the 1660s but died away after 1664 without leaving traces to flow into later legislative procedures. For most of these early sessions—though not all—the assembled legislators were also required to subscribe to an oath of secrecy, which suggests that their records were intended for their own reference only.[7] In Virginia, where numbers but not names were recorded in some divisions in the 1680s, the information could again have been of use only to the members since no one among the electorate could have expected access to the journals.[8] The very rarity even of the practice of recording numbered divisions may well be explained by the fact that the journals were liable to be inspected by the agents of the crown, to whom the burgesses were not anxious to reveal internal divisions.

Other colonial assemblies gave repeated evidence of resenting unauthorized reporting of their proceedings, for which the printers were liable to be punished.[9] They all knew that whenever they came into conflict with the royal or proprietary governor their interests were best protected by the fullest possible appearance of solidarity. Issues of major constitutional importance sometimes made that solidarity impossible to maintain, but when that happened, first in Massachusetts and soon afterward in Maryland, it was evidence of the difficulty of the problem.

The dispute between Governor Shute and the Massachusetts House of Representatives, which began virtually on his arrival in 1716, led to an open difference of opinion as to the governor's powers under the charter. It was as a later result of this controversy that the Privy Council issued the Explanatory Charter. The legislature was asked to agree to an interpretation of the Charter of 1691 which conferred on the governor power to veto the House's choice of Speaker and to determine the duration of the House's sitting. The assembly debate took place in January 1726. The questions were serious enough; but the debate was to have a historic result the character of which was not immediately apparent and which seems to have entirely escaped notice by historians.

The representatives had to face the fact that the Privy Council was claiming authority to interpret the charter. Since to interpret is often to change some existing practice, and certainly to establish one for the future, the constitutional implications were a challenge to the province's oldest prejudices. If any interpreting was to be done, the assembly wished to do it. But it will be recalled that the Privy Council was itself well enough aware of the delicacy of the situation to offer Massachusetts the choice of accepting or rejecting the new clauses. In view of the gravity of this question, which might have led to a complete review of the charter in Britain, the assembly took up a proposal that the Speaker should be requested to ask each member for his opinion separately, the answers to be recorded in the journal. This question was itself debated (though we have no record of what was said) before the House proceeded to the main question of approving the new clauses. The substantive division on acceptance of the Explanatory Charter resulted in an affirmative vote of forty-eight to thirty-two.[10] Within a week, one of the two Boston newspapers had taken a step into history by publishing this division.

The usually unadventurous *Boston News-Letter*, which came the closer to being a court paper, printed the Explanatory Charter together with the assembly's dutiful resolution of acceptance but without reference to a division. But its more enterprising rival, James Franklin's "country" journal, *The New-England Courant*, did far better justice to the occasion by printing the division list in full, names and all. It even supplemented the names of members by adding the towns they represented and, where possible, by adding members' civil or military offices or ranks.[11]

James Franklin had scored a "first" of unusual proportions. For this was the first time in the history of the English-speaking world that an officially recorded legislative division list was published in the press. If we except the oddity of seventeenth-century Maryland, it was the first time that any representative assembly in either England or America had caused a division list to be recorded in its journals. It was not the first time that newspapers had printed unofficial lists, for this had been happening in England in 1722, where Franklin's younger brother Benjamin may have noticed the example; but Benjamin by this time had left for Philadelphia, and the credit must go to James. It was Benjamin, however, as Pennsylvania's official printer, who began the practice of printing division lists in the *Assembly Journal* in 1754.[12] Yet James's remarkable initiative failed to inaugurate a practice. Not until the land bank controversy of 1740–41 did the Massachusetts Assembly again risk recording a division, this time on a motion to forbid "the Persons concerned in the Scheme of John Coleman, Esq." to issue "any Bills or Notes of Hand." The motion was defeated, thirty-seven to forty-nine. The House also recorded the yeas and nays on a motion to supply the treasury with bills of credit, to be retired before the year 1742. This division, which resulted in a heavy defeat for the proposal, was taken only after the governor had rejected a compromise between the two houses.[13]

These divisions, on the rare occasions when they occurred, normally reflected the desire of the minority to record their dissents. In the land bank struggle, where the "opposition" supported the scheme and constituted an assembly majority, they had every reason to make their votes known in contrast to the followers of the "court." Until this crisis, however, the House had generally tended to be united in its conflicts with the governor, and any appearance of internal disunity would obviously have been a tactical disadvantage. The political importance of this position was clearly recognized during the controversy with Governor Burnet over the salary question, when the House adopted a resolution which it then ordered to be printed and distributed to the towns.[14]

Occasionally a pamphleteer probed the protective screen of legislative privacy. In 1739 "Americanus" published a leaflet urging the freeholders of Massachusetts to examine the past behavior of their public officers and asked, "How can any of you be truly represented when you know not the sentiments of those who represent you?"[15] The question indicated the emergence of questions of policy, in contrast to the older convention that the representative was chosen, not for specific opinions or to advance recognized interests but because he could be counted on to be a credit to the community. Differences of sentiment were nothing new in Massachusetts, but the pressing questions of economic policy that afflicted the impoverished province were again coming to mean that the acts of legislators bore consequences for the well-being of the inhabitants. The author of the leaflet knew that his temerity might have consequences for his own well-being; he took the precaution of getting his statement printed in Connecticut. It is at least possible, on the other hand, that this was made necessary because no local printer would take the risk. Such leaflets were extremely rare. No doubt most of the critical scrutiny to which the people subjected their legislators took place in taverns, markets, and meetinghouses and on the walk home. But ten years later a similar leaflet attacked the conduct of the assembly in policies relating to currency; this attack was far more penetrating, analytical, and specific about the names and policies of the members, of whom it listed forty who had voted on this question as well as thirty who had voted to expel one member, James Allen, for contempt. Since this information could not have been obtained from the House *Votes*, it must have been supplied by members of the House or perhaps by the clerk. But it seems more likely that the author was himself a member.[16]

The Massachusetts House furnished its members with copies of the *Votes* and kept the towns informed of its proceedings in the same way. One copy was printed for each member and one for each township.[17] Presumably they were accessible for reading in the meetinghouse. This procedure indicates both that the House felt a duty to make its acts known to the towns and that it intended to keep its own hands on the process. No one else was allowed to inform the public, and even critical comment was risky, as the Boston printer Daniel Fowle discovered in 1754 when he published a highly satirical account of the conduct of the assembly which he called *The Monster of Monsters*. It was in all probability the first thing of its kind in America and for some time seemed likely to prove the last. The House reacted by ordering Fowle to be arrested, interrogated, and imprisoned. When he later sued the Speaker and House officers for damages, the House divided, and could not conceal its division, on the question of whether to pay for the defense from public funds—which it agreed to do.[18]

There was a significant similarity between the principles at stake in Maryland and Massachusetts. Since the early 1720s, some of the leading "country" members of the Maryland assembly had been involved in an angry dispute with the young Lord Baltimore, palatine or proprietor of the province, over the question of the source of Maryland's law. Lord Baltimore claimed that authority to give law was in the nature of the proprietorship; his opponents claimed equal rights with all Englishmen and denied that the proprietor's wishes could supersede the common or statute law of England. Forty years before the quarrel with Parliament, colonial subjects thus asserted equality in terms of British rights.[19] The Maryland Assembly began to print its session laws in 1727 and launched its *Votes and Proceedings* series in 1731. It had already, in the absence of a printer, arranged for publication of *Debates and Proceedings* in Philadelphia in 1725—though "debates" was not meant literally. In a minor replica of the problems that had beset the House of Commons nearly one hundred years earlier, the House declined to open its journals for inspection so as to protect itself against the displeasure of the proprietor.[20] The first vote to print a division list was made on 11 July 1732, appropriately enough after a debate on whether to do so: that is, the first listed division is on whether to print the division list.[21]

The exact context is difficult to reconstruct. *The Maryland Gazette* was experiencing one of its periods of silence, brought about by the absence of William Park, the only printer, from the palatinate; the *House Journals* are uninformative, and surviving letters of members throw no light on the subject. (In Park's absence the governor actually had to get his proclamations printed in Philadelphia.) But we know that Lord Baltimore visited his province early in 1732, and we know that the controversy was unresolved.[22] It seems a plausible inference that members of the assembly wanted to place their names on the record as upholding the supremacy of British law on the occasion of the proprietor's arrival in their midst. But the scanty nature of the records does not permit certainty.

The practice of printing division lists thus begun in Maryland remained episodic for many years but became more frequent in the 1760s. The issues that brought about recorded divisions in the decade or so before the Revolution were generally of local importance, though the perspectives of history reduce them to a different scale. Bills for the speedy recovery of small debts and for confining the growing of flax and hemp to the counties where bounty was paid divided the Maryland House, as did the question: "whether any Housekeeper shall keep more than one Dog without being taxed or not? For more than one dog: 20. For one dog: 26."[23]

A serious constitutional question was also at issue in Jamaica in 1735 when the assembly divided over the introduction of martial law. After the initial motion was carried, "And a motion being thereupon made, that the names of the yeas and noes might be inserted in the journal of this house; and it being agreed to by the several members present," the names on either side were duly entered in the *Journal*.[24]

Where, as in New York, party politics were acutely divisive, they could draw out the lines of communication that led directly from assembly politics to the electorate. During the controversial governorship of William Cosby in the 1730s, the Morrisite opposition learned techniques of party warfare that left their mark on the conventions of legislative procedure. The Morrisites contributed to the use of the press as a weapon of political opposition. More than this, they saw that capital was to be made from opening the debates of the legislature to the public, and on at least one occasion they got the House to vote to throw open its doors. They wanted, moreover, to place their own votes as well as those of their opponents on the record, and in June 1737, the assembly voted to record the names of members voting "aye" and "nay" in divisions.[25]

The New York Assembly in no way differed from others in

its determination to keep control of printing rights. It was the first of all colonial assemblies to authorize the printing of its *Votes*, which it did in 1695, but this was for the use of members, not for general information.[26]

The decision gave no license whatever to the ordinary printer. This was not a matter in which assemblies tended to relax their authority as newspapers became more numerous; in 1753 the printer of *The New York Mercury* was cited to answer for printing without permission certain votes passed in the assembly. And long after the requirement of prior license had disappeared for all ordinary forms of publication, it remained in effect for proceedings of the assembly, which might be printed only with the Speaker's permission. An order to this effect, issued in 1754, was repeated at each session down to the Revolution.[27]

When in the course of periodic quarrels with their governors, the colonial assemblies asserted that the people had a right to know the proceedings of their legislators, they began to give evidence of a trend which would have been difficult to reverse. Thus in 1747 the New York Assembly presented its printer with a painful dilemma when it passed a resolution containing a virulent attack on Governor George Clinton— who retaliated by ordering the printer to refrain from printing them. Turning for guidance to his employers, the printer evoked from them the high-toned resolution, "It is the undoubted Right of the People of this Colony, to know the Proceedings of their Representatives."[28] But the assembly retained the right to decide what part of its proceedings to make known. The people's right to know, which served the assembly well in its moment of need, was nicely balanced and made safe by the assembly's right to decide what to tell them. In effect, the assembly's right to control information was the superior consideration.

An almost identical case occurred a few years later in Pennsylvania, where, during a dispute with Governor William

Denny, the assembly entered into its *Journal* a full statement of the procedure for publication. Governors' speeches and the House's answers "with such Votes as are material," were "for the most part immediately printed in the News-Papers, and thereby made more publick than otherwise they would ever be."[29] During this dispute, the assembly denied a charge that it had kept its proceedings secret from the crown. The episode seems to have had a regressive effect on the development of recorded divisions, which had been introduced only the previous year by the official printer, Benjamin Franklin. This practice now suddenly stopped without explanation. But a reason can be read in the politics of the situation. An assembly locked in strife with the governor cannot have been anxious to reveal its own internal divisions to the public, and in this case the minority would have had no advantage in doing so since they were a branch of the prevailing "Quaker" party. But in 1756 the rift could not be concealed when twenty Quaker members withdrew from the assembly over the question of supplying munitions for the war.[30] The assembly seems to have taken the lesson to heart, and division lists were not published again until 1773.[31]

Unity was even more essential when colonial assemblies began to feel the impact of parliamentary power after the close of the Seven Years' War. But as instructions flowed freely from town meetings to representatives, and as assemblies exhorted their constituents to defiance of British authority, the corporate body of the legislature was obliged in each case to relinquish some of its title to separate and aloof identity. It would become increasingly difficult to maintain that sense of distance in which American assemblies had taken a certain pride in the past.

When assemblies were divided on serious issues, the situation offered two possible courses. Either they could attempt to conceal the division to avoid weakening their negotiating position, whether toward royal (or proprietary) officers or to-

THE GIFT OF GOVERNMENT

ward the people; or the parties to the dispute could appeal
from the House to the public. The latter idea was by no means
new when the Morrisites followed it in New York in the mid-
1730s. But in the inflamed situation developing after the Stamp
Act, the tactic had deeper implications. It appears to have
been Samuel Adams who first grasped these possibilities. Two
Boston newspapers, *The Evening Post* and *The Gazette*, were
used as vehicles for the new device of publishing assembly
division lists as electoral propaganda. The *Post* published a
seemingly simple statement of the names of thirty-two members of the House of Representatives, with the names of their
towns; but this was followed by a gloss suggesting to voters
that they should examine these names with a view to their
conduct over the Stamp Act. The initials over which this
statement appeared were "J. R.," but Governor Bernard had
no doubt that the hand was that of Samuel Adams. In reporting to the Earl of Shelburne, Bernard picked out one phrase:
"A general purgation in both Houses was of absolute necessity."[32] A "purgation" of the lower House could be expected
to lead to the desired results when it came to elect the upper,
so it was naturally the assembly elections to which this original piece of propaganda was directed. As Bernard in time
duly reported, nineteen of these thirty-two lost their seats at
the ensuing election.[33] Earlier in the century this turnover might
have been put down to routine causes; but comparison with
neighboring years suggests that by the 1760s it represented
an unusually high proportion of electoral defeats.

The steep increase in political controversy was widely accompanied by intensified public interest. In Pennsylvania,
where an internal controversy was raging between John Dickinson and Joseph Galloway, and where the province had divided into two broad parties following the conventional
assembly majority and the proprietors, Dickinson took the
unusual and possibly unprecedented step of citing an assembly debate in a newspaper attack on his rival, a move that

carried assembly politics out-of-doors to the people.[34] In Boston, James Otis had drawn on an assembly speech when he published his defense of the conduct of the House of Representatives over the matter of the sloop.[35] Since the speech was presumably Otis's own, the precedent was a shade less significant, and the case differed to the extent that the assembly was engaging the governor, but in each case it was becoming gradually clear that assemblies needed to communicate with the public, not merely on broad rhetorical grounds but by way of convincing them of the importance of specific issues.

Some at least of the people responded with an increased interest in the general character of the representatives, but not all these expressions were directed to the grand question of colonial rights against Britain. "A Countryman," writing in *The Boston Gazette* in 1766, remarked sarcastically that "as a secret I can tell you, that all our oppressors are not on the other side of the Atlantic." This was followed by an accusation that public money had been drawn out of the treasury without a vote and that it was a practice for the General Court to grant large sums of public money to particular persons. This charge was followed by chapter and verse indictments against two public officers, Edmond Trowbridge and Thomas Goldthwait. All this led to the demand that the proceedings of the General Court be opened up, that persons who had taken public money out of the province without the court's authority should be called to account, and that there be "no monopolising of public offices."[36] This last was probably an attack on Hutchinson. But the tenor of the article was such as to cast doubt on the integrity of the elected legislators in general. The author declared that this was his first appearance in print and that he expected it to be his last "unless there is further occasion." The charges of corruption were neither answered nor pursued. But a month or so later, another letter criticized the House for certain resolves respecting the reopening of the courts and asked whether the yeas and nays had been taken on "these interesting votes." Citizens were advised to examine the journals and records "and make proper enquiry into the conduct of those you have instructed."[37]

The rightfulness of this manner of political controversy was by no means clearly established. It did not spill over into other matters and seemed to be confined to imperial issues. But several years later Daniel Leonard in his "Massachusettensis" letters denounced the transmitting of names to *The Gazette* in 1766, which he said was "followed by severe strictures and the most illiberal invectives upon the dissentients." John Adams, in the robes of "Novanglus," replied with an argument which in essentials replicated that recently used by the minority in the debate in the English House of Commons: the people had a legitimate interest in the conduct of their representatives and a consequent right to know how they voted.[38]

In the summer of 1766, Boston town meeting, under Samuel Adams's guiding hand, instructed its representatives to take steps "to make the debates of the house of representatives as public as those of the house of commons of Great Britain."[39] The recognition that Britain enjoyed a more open government than Massachusetts in this important respect is itself not without interest: it imposed on colonial assemblies a special urgency in making their claim to be truly representative. Soon afterward the house duly voted to erect a gallery for the public. Since the outsiders who attended debates would normally be Bostonians, and since most of the representatives came from country towns, the public presence could quickly assume the persuasive force of a mob. It has passed unnoticed by historians that the Virginia House of Burgesses had taken this step two years earlier.[40]

These controversies and the opening of assemblies to public audience were both signs and modes of the transformation overtaking American public life. Representatives were now held accountable to the people not merely for their conduct in regard to local interests but for their stand on the newly emerging concept of an American interest. As colonial spokesmen struggled to enunciate a set of principles consistent both with their British rights and with accustomed legislative liberties, they began to forge an American version of the concept of the "whole nation." Colonial leaders found that they had become revolutionary leaders. And as they applied in practice the abstract theory that legitimate government arose from the consent of the governed, consent itself became an increasingly active principle, and the old convention of legislative privacy began to crumble. It was tainted with the same odor as toryism, aristocracy, and oligarchy.

The Revolution became, among other things, a revolution in America in the relations between rulers and ruled, as Gordon Wood has ably argued.[41] The emerging attitudes, which were permeated with a profound distrust of power and an ingrained suspicion of the motives of men in public office, could not be confined to the general American hostility to the power of Britain. They were soon reflected throughout the new state constitutions. Everywhere it was ordained that assembly journals were to be accessible to public inspection; and although state constitutions differed on the question of public access, it became customary to admit the public to debates.[42]

The states in turn were represented by their delegations at the Continental Congress, which chose to deliberate in secret. Charles Thomson, the secretary of the Congress, used the local press as his medium for communicating congressional decisions to the people, a method which could easily seem either patronizing or parochial. The duties of members of the Congress kept them extremely busy. But they do not always seem to have realized that the American public was in need of information, guidance, and encouragement. In May 1777, Thomas Jefferson complained to John Adams about the general lack of information coming from the Congress. The Maryland Assembly soon began to worry about its delegates' fidelity to state interests on the vital issue of western land, for which cause Maryland held up the ratification of the Articles of Confederation until 1781, and it was for this reason, on Maryland's instigation, that the Congress instituted the practice of keeping a record of its roll calls.[43]

When the Continental Congress first decided to keep its deliberations secret, the policy caused neither surprise nor any significant complaint. The delegates' immediate reasons were probably tactical; it was not desirable that disagreements within the Congress should become public knowledge. The importance of this policy increased as the Congress involved itself in much inherently confidential business, including the establishment of committees to negotiate with foreign powers; meanwhile, the many deep divisions, personal animosities, and manifestations of distrust that forced their way into the light of daily debate would have impaired the credibility of the Congress both at home and, just as seriously, abroad.

But this process could not be checked. Bitter internal disputes, and particularly the feud between Arthur Lee and Silas Deane, could not be kept between the walls. Secrecy in these circumstances increased suspicion. "A True Patriot" asked in *The Pennsylvania Gazette* whether Congress knew what became of public money; could the greater part of it be accounted for? "The *strict secrecy* which Congress seems to enjoin on its Members with respect to almost all its business is by no means calculated to remove the conceived suspicions." This and many similar criticisms coming to a head in 1779 destroyed much of the respect in which the Congress had been held. In July 1780, the Virginia House of Delegates adopted a resolution criticizing the Congress for lapses in the publication of the yeas and nays in its records. This complaint was made possible because Congress in August 1777 had adopted a rule that any member could request the yeas and nays, which were to be recorded in the *Journal*. But the concession to

American public opinion which events in 1779 had forced out of Congress still did not amount to a thoroughly reformed conception of the nature of the relationship. Difficulties appeared from any direction in which the Congress turned. Gouverneur Morris put the dilemma at the height of a dispute over fisheries: "It is peculiarly unfortunate for the People and for Congress that Subjects of this Sort should be thus publickly agitated. Without divulging the Secrets of Congress it is impossible to place the Subject in its proper Light and yet unless that is done the People will probably be deluded and if it is done Congress must become contemptible abroad and consequently insignificant at home."[44]

The habits of generations did not fall lightly from American shoulders. If the Revolution produced changed relations between ruler and ruled, it also produced many new rulers who seem to have been willing to slip into the mantles worn by their predecessors. The two episodes in the history of American constitutional privacy which are well enough known to form part of the stock of common historical knowledge still lay in the future when American independence had been secured. The first of these was the profound secrecy of the Constitutional Convention held at Philadelphia in 1787; the second was the early policy of the United States Senate of meeting in secret and not disclosing its debates to the public.

The Constitutional Convention's decision to deliberate in secret occasioned no internal debate and does not seem to have been controversial with the wider public. When the draft constitution came to be debated by state conventions, the Anti-Federalists mustered every available argument against it. Both the motives and the judgment of the constitution-makers were called in question by a wide range of critics. But the secrecy of their debates played little or no part in this barrage of criticism.[45] The concept of the people's right to know had not yet made its way as a commonplace into political discourse, and it is an interesting comment that although the proceedings of state legislatures were by this time getting into the newspaper press, the higher level of responsibility involved in the making of a constitution—or, as was generally supposed, in amending of the existing Articles—seems to have remained under the traditional protection. The propriety of this decision also raises interesting questions. Most Americans have, historically, been reasonably satisfied with their Constitution. Yet it is very doubtful whether they would have had the Constitution if the debates of the convention had been subject to daily comment and the views of members had been subject to the pressure of local criticism while the document was in process of being framed. Once the instrument of government lay before them, the people through their state conventions could consider it on its merits, as a whole. But that whole represented a series of complex agreements, compromises, and concessions which could hardly have been achieved in a forum open to the country. The best open covenants are not always those that have been openly arrived at.

The mood had changed by the time of the ratifying conventions. Massachusetts, New York, Pennsylvania, and Virginia employed or permitted stenographers to record the actual debates, and these were duly published both in the press and in authorized volumes. But this reporting of debates was itself a recent phenomenon in American public affairs and brings us to notice the most curious feature in the history of the relationship—a long one by this time—between American representative assemblies and their constituents. The phenomenon has perhaps been difficult for historians to discern because it consists of silence. Nowhere and at no time in the history of the colonies did any newspaper or magazine report one single assembly debate. We have noticed a few fragmentary exceptions when speeches made in assemblies were cited in the course of political polemics. But these were individual speeches, not debates, and do not constitute an exception to the rule. Americans were well aware that speeches in both

Houses of Parliament were often reported in the English newspapers from which colonial printers frequently copied them. Since the speeches reprinted in American newspapers were nearly always those of members who took the American standpoint, they were in fact an important source of the prevalent but misguided belief that British sentiment was generally sympathetic to the colonies.[46] Colonial editors were therefore certainly aware that such communication was possible. In view of the general exclusion of visitors from the legislative chambers of America—Virginia and Massachusetts only made a beginning in the mid-1760s—it would have been necessary to secure special permission for the presence of a reporter, but there is no evidence that this was ever sought.[47]

The silence of the colonial press is a real loss to historians, though it is one which in the nature of the case has seldom been noticed. The debates that must have taken place over the question of constitutional power in Boston in 1726 and over the land bank repeal in 1741 were only two that might have thrown light on the problems of colonial interpretations of their constitutional relationship to Britain. But it is not only a question of getting information about moments of drama. P. D. G. Thomas has pointed out that the parliamentary opposition to Walpole, and later to North, did not overthrow these statesmen by the sheer force of any single argument. The effect was cumulative.[48] They were gradually weakened and undermined by a steady and rising flow of parliamentary criticism in protracted debates. What we miss in the colonial scene is not so much the account of any one dramatic debate as the tones and trends that mark the changing mood of a period.

One partial explanation of this silence must be considered as reflecting the practical possibilities of the colonial printer's enterprise. To have kept a reporter in the assembly chamber all day during the session would have been expensive and probably beyond their means. They could, however, have provided an outlet for members who wanted their speeches published, but this was not done either. In general, it appears that the demand did not exist. No doubt some of what passed in the assembly got around in the taverns and markets; much of it may have been regarded as familiar. The explanation that lies beyond these considerations must reach into the difference between Britain's metropolitan political culture and the provinciality of the colonies, which were in many ways genuine provinces of Britain. Politics is a form of theater, and the House of Commons was the world's greatest political stage. Although Philadelphia was one of the most populous cities in the British Empire, it had no magnetism remotely comparable to that of London. It does not seem to have occurred to America's colonial legislators that they might have addressed themselves to a wider audience or that future generations would have liked to read their words.

It was not until after the War of Independence, with all its furious internal controversies, that the Irish immigrant printer Mathew Carey first brought to America the idea of reproducing assembly debates. On 29 October 1785, Carey opened the columns of his *Pennsylvania Evening Herald* to reports of debates in the state assembly. The subjects of discussion were the election of the Speaker and the question of whether a certain member had been duly returned. Clearly, it was not the intrinsic importance of the issues but the general interest attaching to legislative proceedings that moved Carey to this experiment.

A few days later Carey presented a petition to be allowed to sit "within the bar" so as better to be able to hear the debates for the purpose of reporting them. In the discussion that ensued—and which he duly reported—no member objected to the principle of reporting. Robert Morris was typical in saying that he thought it "very proper that the constituents should be made acquainted with the proceedings of their representatives." If Carey's petition presented a problem, it was rather that members did not wish his reports to have the im-primatur of official status. After all, his reporting might be selective and might or might not be entirely accurate. For these reasons, members preferred to let Carey take his place with-out giving him any form of official sanction. The adjournment of this debate without a formal decision therefore seems to represent a decision to that effect.[49]

Carey followed up his own initiative by collecting the Pennsylvania Assembly debates on the bill to repeal the char-ter of the Bank of North America, then at the center of the state's political conflict, and making them available in pamph-let form for the benefit of the common reader. He found it necessary to explain in a preface that this novel enterprise was entirely free from any political bias. His method did jus-tice to both sides. What Carey was doing was to advance—if not actually to introduce—the concept of impartial political reporting by the newspaper itself, as opposed to the usual practice in American newspapers of *receiving* reports from a variety of correspondents while keeping the columns open to different views. Carey went to some length to explain the care taken to ensure the accuracy of his notes. The public would receive a straightforward report of the debate.[50]

Carey, who had previously reported debates in the Dublin Parliament, was right in his estimate that Americans were ready for the same enterprise and must have been pleased to find that the field was open. Within a few months the practice was copied by other papers in Philadelphia, in New York, and in Connecticut.[51] In the early stages the writers had to find their way to a proper literary mode of presentation for this material. A report in *The New York Journal*, for example, began by observing that a full account of the debate in the assembly would fill twelve columns, to reproduce all of which would be a "futile misspence of time." The reporter then gave a partly impressionistic account, distributing honors with reasonable fairness among the participants, of whom the most prominent was Alexander Hamilton.[52] It seems a little curious that readers in Massachusetts had to wait until their state's ratifying convention before they were able to read a report of the debate in their own newspapers, the first of which appeared in *The Boston Gazette* on 4 February 1788.

The creation of a new national government elevated and broadened the stage of politics. Newspaper printers grasped the opportunity. When John Fenno launched his *Gazette of the United States* in 1790, he at once announced his intention of bringing the debates of Congress before the public, a purpose fulfilled in subsequent issues; Philip Freneau adopted the same policy with the *National Gazette* nineteen months later.[53] For these ventures the people of New York, then Philadelphia, constituted the immediate readership, although they were intended to exert wider influence on American opinion. These readers were the same people who had resided in those cities only two years earlier. But they were now the people of a new federal republic; they were citizens under a government operating on a national scale and on a national stage. This was by no means the beginning of a national politics, but it was the beginning of a *theater* of national politics.

In the light of all these accumulating events, the decision of the first Senate of the United States to hold its deliberations in secret may well have appeared regressive. That such a decision was still possible provides powerful evidence of the inertial force of the habit of privacy. The people's interest in knowing their legislators' proceedings was certainly by this time a preference; it might still have been premature to have called it a right. It seems probable that the senators justified their decision to themselves on the ground that they were answerable primarily to their states, not to the people at large. The practice endured for four years. It then broke down, partly because the Senate had to debate an issue which did seem to require public access. When Albert Gallatin presented his credentials to the first session of the third Congress, he was challenged on the ground that he had not been a citizen of the United States long enough to meet the qualifications. The Senate decided to conduct this inquiry in public. To have done otherwise might have aroused dark suspicions that a small oligarchy was setting up an exclusive membership. Both the debate and the outcome, which was unfavorable to Gallatin, were fully reported without comment in the press.[54]

Even before the Gallatin case had been decided, the Senate opened its doors to the public for all ordinary debates. The resolution that carried the day declared that the senators owed equal responsibility to the powers by which they were appointed "as if that body were derived immediately from the people." The language suggests that a point of principle had been established.[55]

The struggles of the newspaper writers were not entirely finished. When the House of Representatives first debated the seating of reporters it was merely on the matter of audibility, not of principle. (William Laughton Smith of South Carolina had seen reports giving "accounts" for "acts" and "barbers" for "harbours.") There was also some slight concern not to give preference to any particular newspaper. The Speaker was given discretion to provide seating space for the reporters.[56] A practice had been established, but not a right, and when the Congress convened for the first time in Washington the question had to be reconsidered if only because the physical arrangements were now less convenient. Several reporters petitioned to be allowed to sit "within the bar" to be better placed to hear the speeches. Even now, the committee to whom this request was referred came back with a recommendation "that it is not expedient that the House should take any order on the memorial presented." There seems to have been a good deal of feeling that the reporters were so inaccurate that members could hardly recognize their own sentiments and that for this reason their activities should not be encouraged; but other members drew the opposite inference, that they should be given better facilities. No one admitted to dissenting from the now generally recognized view that the people had a right to know their legislator's proceedings; but it is possible to guess that some members might still have preferred privacy under some other guise. The House divided equally, forty-five on each side, and with the Speaker voting with the committee, no action was taken. It appears that the reporters had to be content with their places in the gallery.[57] As late as January 1802, the printer of *The Washington Federalist* apologized to readers for not having known "that liberty was granted to Stenographers to take a stand in the Senate" and promised to report debates in both houses.[58]

Neither political representation nor popular government was a new idea at the time of the American Revolution. What was new in the politics of the time was the use of representation as a clearly defined institutional bridge between people and government. The two-way traffic over this bridge was a traffic in knowledge. The men who devised the Constitution and the men who wrote the *Federalist Papers* had not anticipated that the principle of accountability would assume forms that would subject it to such intimate, yet public, investigation and control. A politics of trust was replaced by a politics of vigilance. It was a legitimate adaptation to the experience of the times, and in the changing political expectations of those times it was a change that in turn established a new condition of political legitimacy. Only through knowledge of the government of America could the people confide to it their confidence and trust.

CHAPTER SIX

Government
and Happiness

Two different but superficially similar modes of thought about political representation have taken historical shape under the cover of the same institutions. It is to this continuity of institutions that they owe their appearance of similarity. Under the older regime, the representative body stood aloof from the people but often in a state of defiance against the crown or its agents. There is nothing incongruous about calling this system, in which the legislature stands independent of those it represents, a system of representation. It was in virtue of their *representative* character that legislators could be entrusted with affairs of state and could meet together as equals, free from any threat of external interference. The second, and as far as we are concerned, more familiar system, however, assumes a closer and more continuous nexus between legislators and people. By virtue, again, of being the people's representatives, the legislators are now obliged to keep the people informed of their conduct and their votes, from which it follows that the people may not only judge them at the end of a session but may form their opinions on every day's news.

When the differences between the two systems are stated in this manner, the historical differences stand out more clearly than was true to the circumstances of historical change. The truth is that no linear process of transition can be traced from the earlier to the later. The intense excitement of the early 1640s generated a sudden outburst of interest in parliamentary affairs, flooding over the old boundaries of legislative privacy, a process which served to teach the House of Commons to keep guard against intrusions from below as well as above. Party warfare and public interest were pitched at new intensities under William and Anne. Parliament was no longer the representative of its separate constituencies; but the idea that it represented the "whole nation," which gradually took effective root in these very years, growing to overshadow the land in Walpole's oligarchy, showed no disposition to compromise with the doctrine of continuous accountability. Parliamentary accountability to the people, when it cropped up, was a product of the politics of discontent.

It is far from surprising that the colonial assemblies, with their intense parliamentary self-consciousness, should have taken similar courses. They too faced periodic threats from royal agents. Although their independence was no more threatened by popular discontent than was that of Parliament itself, they were careful to protect themselves against encroachments on their privacy or their dignity from any quarter. There is a very natural temptation to adopt a form of geometrical symbolism when comparing the colonial assemblies with Parliament. Was their development, if not exactly in phase with that of the House of Commons, at least in parallel? But once we have disposed of the idea of linear development, such geometrical analogies are irrelevant. Two nonlinear processes cannot be conceived of as parallel.

The colonial assemblies in their different ways adapted themselves to changing circumstances in a manner that was fairly consistently closer to their origins than could be said of Parliament. Forms of government changed in Massachusetts with the new Charter of 1691 and with the Explanatory Char-

ter of 1725–26; in Pennsylvania with the charter wrested from
William Penn in 1701; and in a few other instances when control passed to or from the crown. But these events were rare.
In general the colonies lived under remarkably stable systems, and those systems absorbed and responded to the pressure generated by economic, social, and religious change
without much visible alteration.

At irregular intervals, and with little sign of consistent purpose, the assemblies did enlarge their grasp. The rise of the
assembly is a phenomenon not seriously to be contested. Yet
this rise took place on a very firm original foundation; it was
a development, and this point is of cardinal importance, that
was seen and held to be wholly consistent and, when accom-
plished, actually continuous with the character of their original foundation. J. G. A. Pocock has recently observed that
the United States returned to first principles because there
was nowhere else to go;[1] but it would be closer to the truth to
say that the Americans stayed with their first principles because they had never been anywhere else. The assemblies of
New England continued to meet as they had always met, every
year, after new elections; so did that of Pennsylvania. Those
of other colonies, elected at varying intervals, had known no
interruption to their regular proceedings other than the period of the Dominion of New England and the interlude of
government without assembly in Virginia from 1706 to 1710.
The institutional history of the United States owes much of
its dense complexity to the difficulties of making institutions
derived from first principles work through the accretions of
generations of change and growth; but that is a story which
reflects most specifically on the doctrine of the separation of
powers. At the time of the American Revolution the colonial
struggle with Parliament was viewed very clearly and with
intense passion as a struggle of conflicting principles. The
irony of this conflict lay in the fact that the contestants on
both sides claimed to derive their authority from the same

source. But with the colonies the claim to *ideological* consistency was much the more intense and, moreover, had the better historical foundation. Colonists had never admitted any interruption to their principles because—with the rare exceptions noted—they had never experienced any interruption of their practices. From their point of view the regime of Andros was illegal. While in England no parliament was called from 1629 to 1640, and parliaments persisted into uninterrupted if fretful longevity under both Cromwell and Charles II, colonial assemblies continued to answer to the normal rhythm of their electoral authority.

When Lawrence Stone calls the England of the triennial parliaments, from 1694 to 1716, "a genuine participatory democracy," he reflects the modern historian's habitual tendency to overestimate the extent to which Parliament could really be equated with government.[2] Parliament was emerging as an irreversible force in early eighteenth-century Britain. The long wars contributed very materially to the circumstances which brought parliaments forward into the mechanism of government. But before the Septennial Act of 1716 it would have been almost impossible to foresee that the rapid rise of private interests would convert Parliament, and particularly the House of Commons, into a principal agent of economic change and political policy.

Under the pressure of these forces, Parliament became the true voice and agency of the interests of property: not only the landed estates of old but the new property of commerce, of the law, and of the wealth of the East and West Indies. While Parliament legislated itself into a positively less democratic relationship to the nation, the political and economic nation changed in character; in its own turn Parliament, and especially the House of Commons, found within its existing structure and on the foundation of its unreformed constituency the means to become substantially representative of the new interests that were creating the new wealth and power of the nation. That is the fundamental reason why the Parliament of Great Britain averted reform throughout the age of European revolution.

The nation, conceived in its broadest sense, extended to include the empire. The institutions of Britain and of Britain's colonies formed part of a whole. Parliament and assemblies were elements in a single system, loosely-knit, poorly coordinated, and lacking any comprehensive theory save that of indivisible sovereignty; but all, within the orbits of their own range of powers and given responsibilities, responded to similar forces. It was when the orbits intersected and when Parliament and assemblies asserted for themselves portions of the authority already claimed by the others that the single system split into two; it could well have split into many more parts. Parliament insisted on its character as a government, making laws and directing policy and extending increasingly into every corner of the colonies. These claims were fully consistent with and in a very true sense representative of the needs of an expanding Britain. But to the inhabitants of the colonies they represented a comparatively new phenomenon, for which authority was dubious and precedent obscure. It is altogether to be expected that the record should reveal the colonies encountering these claims with doubt and differences of opinion before hardening into hostility. Colonists hoped constantly for a return to the old ways under which they had grown and prospered and which they felt they understood. No one in America had any desire to elaborate a thoroughly self-consistent theory. It could probably not be done. Certainly it could be done only by subjecting some part of the empire to an intolerable strain. When Britain enforced the theory of indivisible sovereignty it was the colonial assemblies that felt the strain. None of them could have met the challenge alone, and eventually they contrived to meet it instead by a new form of representative institution, the Continental Congress.

Such a crisis called the foundations of government into question. Jefferson affirmed, and the Congress adopted his words, that governments long established should not be changed for light and transient causes; but these causes were not light nor did they seem likely to be transient, since Americans believed that the causes threatened to change the character of their own government from liberty to slavery. The nature of the contest therefore called for a searching return to first principles. In this sense it may be said that Americans discovered the truth of the doctrine of *redurri ai principii* that Machiavelli had laid down as essential to the survival of republics.

A very sophisticated legal language had grown around these principles. The problem of the lawyer—or of the politician making use of the laws—was to express his client's interest in language that carried conviction in legal terms. But the problem of the philosopher was to cut away the encrustations of law to get straight at the real interests of the people involved in any particular dispute. The quarrel between Britain and her colonies broke out at a time when an increasingly explicit form of utilitarian philosophy was affecting people's ideas about the objects of government. But before the greatest happiness of the greatest number could be propounded as the highest good, the idea of happiness had itself to gain a respectable footing on the ground previously occupied by great principles owing their historic sanctity to patriarchal and providential purposes. The American Puritans were the last people who would have wished to reduce these aims to merely material terms; and they did their best to uphold some version of the godly commonwealth after England had gone down the slippery path of religious toleration. But in New England as in England, Scotland, and indeed in the other American colonies, the idea of happiness was being gradually transmuted into a cost-accounted standard of human benefits. Eighteenth-century ministers of religion, reconciling themselves to conditions of a prosperity earned by hard work and sanctioned by divine benevolence, came to dwell on the idea of happiness with increasingly complacent indulgence. In this process the word acquired a more material significance. When a seventeenth-century minister talked about the happiness of a people—at that time still a comparatively uncommon mode of speech—he meant their freedom to serve Christ; for it was in the service of Christ that the only true happiness was to be found. But we can see all this changing as the ministers who find themselves surrounded by prosperous or aspiring merchants and farmers talk more as though happiness could be attained not by the people but by people, as individuals, through the gratification of their own desires.

The word was under some strain in the period of the American Revolution—the strain felt in undergoing a transmutation from one meaning to another while keeping the same outward form. The first edition of the *Encyclopaedia Britannica*,[3] published in 1771, gave it only a couple of lines, with the observation that among philosophers it meant the pursuit of some good; this bore traces of the older type of belief, abstract, general, and probably of theological origin. The good could more easily be understood in a religious context, or in that of some grand design of human improvement, than as pertaining to a rabble of individuals lunging for private gain. Samuel Johnson's *Dictionary* offered a variety of readings from different authors, suggesting both spiritual and personal aims without proposing any particular preferences. When Thomas Jefferson snatched the word out of the air of the age in which he lived, he united natural rights philosophy (which Bentham despised) with the well-being of the people as a whole; but at the same time his usage hinted at the legitimacy of personal aspirations linked to the enjoyment of individual life and liberty.

The expression was fraught with the resonance of a very respectable past. Jefferson had no idea of introducing a new justification for the purposes of government.[4] If human nature—of which American nature was a possibly superior example—aspired to happiness, then men had created government to protect and advance those aspirations, to the somewhat limited extent that government could do such things without itself becoming a menace to liberty. The gift that government could offer and which it owed to the people by these terms of reckoning was not fundamentally different in an America secure in the sunshine of natural rights from what it was in a Britain breathing the coarse air of utilitarianism. But government operated under license. It owed its just powers to the consent of the governed. The gift of legitimate authority for government itself was ultimately tested in the happiness of the people.

In Britain, and the rest of Europe, such a view was confined to a skeptical minority; but it was more than a mere philosophical plaything, as many governments were to find in the next half-century of revolution. Its more truly revolutionary meaning, however, was first proved in America.

Appendix

The Pennsylvania Evening Herald and the American Monitor. Printed by
M. Carey & Co. (Philadelphia). No. 31, Wednesday,
November 9, 1785.

Report of the debates of the Assembly of Pennsylvania for Monday,
November 7, P.M.

[p. 124, second page of the issue]

Mr. Finlay said, as the petition of Mathew Carey, praying leave to sit within
the bar, for the purpose of taking the debates, was on the files of the house,
it was necessary that it should be disposed of in some manner. He had con-
versed with many of the members on the subject, and they had all appeared
to have no objection to allowing him a situation provided there was no entry
relative to it made on the minutes. He therefore thought that the best mode
would be to let the speaker exert his privilege in this case—which would
render it easy, if the indulgence was abused, to put an end to it, without
requiring the interference of the house.

It was here moved, that the petition be read a second time, which was
done accordingly.

Mr. Smiley moved that the prayer of said petition be granted.

Mr. R. Morris had no objection to mr. Carey's taking notes of the debates;
and publishing them. —On the contrary, he thought it very proper that the
constituents should be made acquainted with the proceedings of their representatives. —But he was sorry the petition had been pressed forward—as
it would be highly improper to authorize a person by a vote of the house, to
publish their proceedings, when not subject to their inspection. Coming under that sanction, they would be esteemed as warranted by their authority.
And if there was any disagreement between them and the records of the
clerks, the house would be held responsible. At the conclusion of the petition, there was mention made of the parliamentary debates in England and
Ireland. —As this seemed to convey an idea, that the indulgence prayed for,
was accorded there, he had made some enquiry, and found, that far from
this being the case, any person observed taking notes in the lobby there,

149

particularly in England, was liable to be turned out. —Mr. Morris here moved that the further consideration of the petition be postponed.

Mr. Smiley. The gentleman has made mention of the practice in England: but the genius of our government is widely different. There, they sometimes have their doors open—at other times shut. Any member ·can at any time order the galleries to be cleared. The framers of our constitution have ordered that our doors shall be kept constantly open, unless when the welfare of the state requires otherwise. This being the case, we cannot hinder mr. Carey from taking notes outside the bar. It is therefore clearly our interest to afford him every possible convenience for printing the debates as accurately as possible. It appears to be the joint sense of both sides of the house, that the indulgence be granted—the only question that arises, is, with respect to the mode. —If any gentleman has any plan to propose, to obviate the objections relative to sanctioning it by vote, I shall readily withdraw the petition.

Mr. Fitzsimons took up the same ground of argument that mr. Morris had made use of. —He had no objection to the permission, provided it were granted without the sanction of a vote. —He was not clear that a situation within the bar afforded greater opportunity for hearing than one without. — He concluded with remarking that the house of assembly had an equal privilege with the English house of commons, to clear the gallery whenever the welfare of the state might require.

Mr. Smiley replied that there was an essential difference; as here it must be proved that the welfare of the state rendered the caution necessary—but in England it entirely depended on the will of each individual, without assigning any reason.

Mr. Finley spoke a second time to enforce what he had already advanced, as did messrs. Fitzsimons and Morris, when at length, the question being put, mr. Morris's motion for postponement was carried.

Adjourned.

On the following pages is a facsimile of the issue of The New-England Courant *(15–22 January 1726) in which for the first time in the history of the English-speaking world an officially recorded legislative division list was reported in the press. The report begins on the front page, near the bottom of the second column. Courtesy of Readex Microprint Corporation.*

FOREIGN AFFAIRS.

London, July 10.

ON Monday, the 28th past, came on the Election of a Burgess for Bodmin in Cornwall : The Candidates were the Hon. Mr. West, Lord Chancellor of Ireland, and John Laroche, Esq; an Exempt of his Majesty's Yoemen of the Guards ; and the former had the Majority by one Vote.

We hear that the South Sea Company have receiv'd Advice, that their 12 Greenland Ships have already had such good Success, that they have taken about 45 Whales.

Near 30 of the late Mr. Guy's Relations are come to London from Staffordshire, to receive their respective Legacies from the Corporation appointed by Act of Parliament to put his Will in Execution.

Mr. John Morris who kept the Bull-Inn in Leadenhall-street, having receiv'd Advice from the Country on Tuesday Night of the Death of his Wife, shot himself last Wednesday Morning, and dy'd immediately.

On Thursday the Astronomical Works of of the late Revd. Mr. Flamstead, his Majesty's Astronomer, entitled *Historia Cælestis Britannica*, were presented to his Royal Highness the Prince at Richmond, as they were likewise to his Majesty just before his Departure for Hanover, and were very graciously receiv'd.

The Society for propagating the Gospel in the North of Scotland which was incorporated by a Charter of Queen Ann about the beginning of her Reign, and for which a thousand Pounds was then contributed, has since met with such wonderful Encouragement by the Generosity and Charity of several Gentlemen, that their Capital is now increased to 10,000 l. with the Interest of which they pay between 60 and 70 School-masters, who daily teach about 24000 Boys and Girls in those Parts. His Majesty, when he heard of the prudent and honest Management of the Society, was so pleas'd that about two Months ago he gave them 1200 l. a Year out of the Civil List for employing itinerant Ministers to preach the Gospel.

Dresden. July 10. The Letters from

Warsaw mention a Story which certainly cannot meet with Credit from any but such as are offuscated with the grossest Superstition, viz. That a certain Protestant Prince, whom they do not think fit to name, riding out on Horse back to take the Air, with a small Retinue, happen'd to meet a Romish Priest, who had the Host hid under his Gown, which he said he was going to carry to a Person who was dangerously ill ; and that the Prince being so curious as to press that he might see it, the Priest took out the Wafer-Box, whereupon the Prince's Horse, more religious it seems than his Master, fell on his Knees, so that the Prince with all his whiping and spurring could not get him upon his Legs, till the Priest was gone.

Hague, July 20. On the 30th ult. we receiv'd Letters from Rome, which say that the Pope going to visit Father Ripoly, the new General of the Order of Dominicans, kneel'd down to him, and kiss'd his Hand with a profound Humility, becoming the Servant of the Servants of God, thereby acknowledging him as his Superior, and General of his Order. On the Eve of St. Peter and St. Paul, the Pope being at St. Peter's Church, Constable Colonna, Ambassador Extraordinary from the Emperor for that Purpose, made the usual Present of the Nag to the Pope, by way of Tribute, for the Kingdom of Naples ; but his Holiness would not suffer the Beast to set a Foot within the Church. The same Letters say, that as the Pope was going into the Cathedral, a Person stood near the Holy Water-Pot, who being possess'd with the Devil, made a terrible Howling, and was miserably distorted, but that the Pope no sooner pronounced the Blessing, than the Person became silent, and fell down as it were dead, which made the Sanders-by cry out, A Miracle ! The Advices from thence seem positive, that the Pope is contriving an Alliance betwixt the Emperor and the King of Spain and Portugal, with a View to procure a firm Support to the Romish Religion against its Adversaries.

Boston, January 15.
From the Votes of the House of Representatives. Sabbati Die 15 *Januarij,* 1725.

The House Entred into the further Consideration of His Majesty's Royal Explanatory Charter, and after some debate being had thereon, The House Resolved, That the Question should be put to each Member present, who should declare his Acceptance

151

er Non-Acceptance thereof by his saying Yea or Nay, and Mr. Speaker did accordingly put the Question to each Member present, who severally declared for themselves as appears by the List hereafter following, Viz.

[N.B. *The Military Titles, &c. of some of the Members, and Names of the Towns which they represent, omitted in the Votes, are here added.*]

Yeas.	Towns Names.
Maj. Thomas Tileston	Dorchester
Lieut. Joshua Fisher	Dedham
Lieut. Robert Blake	Wrentham
Col. John Chandler Esq;	Woodstock
Timothy Lindal Esq;	Salem
Capt. Daniel Epes	Salem
John Wainwright Esq;	Ipswich
Capt. Henry Rolfe	Newbury
Capt. Jeremiah Stevens	Salisbury
Mr. John Hovie	Topsfield
Mr. Samuel Stevens	Gloucester
Mr. Jonathan Raymont	Beverly
Jonathan Remington Esq; Judge of Probate	Cambridge
Henry Phillips Esq;	Charlstown
Mr. Joseph Lemmon	Charlstown
Jonas Bord Esq;	Watertown
Mr. William Wilson	Concord
Mr. Caleb Rice	Marlborough
Capt. John Shipley	Groton
Lieut. Thomas Bancroft	Reading
Capt. Joseph Lablancgroue	Lexington
Lieut. Josiah Jones	Weston
Col. Eleazer Tyng Esq;	Dunstable
Capt. Isaac Powers	Littleton
Lieut. William Puncheon	Springfield
Capt. John Stoddard Esq;	Northampton
Lieut. Westwood Cooke	Hadley
Henry Dwight Esq;	Hatfield
John Ashley Esq;	Westfield
Capt. Thomas Wells	Deerfield
Capt. Benjamin Warren, Indian Justice	Plymouth
Mr. John Kent	Marshfield
Mr. Samuel Sprague	Duxbury
Mr. Thomas Turner	Rochester
Ezra Bourn Esq;	Sandwich
Mr. John Snow	Truro
Col. Nathaniel Paine Esq;	Bristol
Capt. Seth Williams Esq; Judge	Taunton
Mr. Ephraim Pierce	Swansey
Ensign Joseph Peck	Rehoboth
Thomas Church Esq;	Little Compton
Capt. John Foster	Attleborough
Lieut. Thomas Terrey Esq;	Freetown
Capt. Nicholas Shapleigh	Kittery
Mr. Dependence Littlefield	Wells
Capt. James Grant	Berwick
Major Samuel Moodey	Falmouth
The Honourable William Dudley Esq; Speaker.	Roxbury

48

Nays.	Towns Names.
Mr. Isaiah Tay	
William Clark Esq;	
Mr. Ezekiel Lewis	Boston
Mr. Thomas Cushing	
Mr. John Wadsworth	Milton
Major John Quincy Esq;	Braintrey
Mr. John Torrey	Weymouth
Capt. Thomas Loring	Hingham
Mr. John Brown	Mendon
Mr. Edward White	Brookline
Mr. John Sanders	Haverill
Ensign John Hobson	Rowley
Mr. Benjamin Barker	Andover
Mr. Joseph Hale	Boxford
Mr. Samuel Tenay	Bradford

Capt. William Rogers	Wenham
Mr. Joseph Davis	Almsbury
Mr. Richard Ward	Newtown
Mr. John Rice	Sherbourn
Capt. Samuel Hullard	Sudbury
Mr. Joseph Wilder	Lancaster
Capt. Edward Goddard	Framingham
Mr. John Blanchard	Billerica
Mr. Daniel Pierce	Woburn
Mr. Jonathan Sergent	Malden
Ensign Samuel Chamberlain	Chelmsford
Mr. Thomas Bryant	Scituate
Mr. Nathanial Southworth	Middleborough
Lieut. Isaac Cushman	Plympton
Mr. Edward Shove	Dighton
Mr. William Stone	Norton

32

Post Meridiem.

Whereas His Honour the Lieut. Governour hath laid before this Court in their present Session for their Acceptance, an Explanatory Charter, received from his Grace the Duke of New-Castle, with a Copy of His Majesty's Order in Council concerning the same, wherein His Majesty hath been pleased to confirm the Charter Granted by their late Majesty's King William and Queen Mary, in which former Charter there being no Express mention made relating to the Choice of a Speaker, and the House's Power of Adjourning, as to both which Points in the Explanatory Charter his Majesty hath been pleased to give particular Direction: We His Majesty's Loyal and Dutiful Subjects being very desirous to Signalize Our Duty and Obedience, which we at all times Owe to His most Excellent Majesty, have and do hereby Accept of the said Explanatory Charter, and shall Act in Conformity thereto for the future, not doubting but that thereby we shall recommend His Majesty's Loyal and Faithful Subjects the Inhabitants of this Province to his further most Gracious Favour and Protection.

Sent up for Concurrence.

Four Gentlemen of the Council, viz. Nathanael Byfield Esq; John Clark Esq; Elisha Cook Esq; and Thomas Palmer Esq; voted against the said Charter, and the rest for it.

Custom-House Boston, January 15.

Entered Inwards. None.

Cleared Out.

Battersby for Glascow, Trout for West Indies, and Bonner for London.

Entered Out.

Compton for Bermuda, Cowhird for Virginia, Kingston for St. Kitts, Tobin for Nevis, and Legard for Barbadoes.

BOSTON: Printed and sold by BENJAMIN FRANKLIN in Union-Street, where Advertisements and Letters are taken in. Price 4 d. single, or 12 s. a Year.

Notes

Chapter One. Political Authority
from Divine Right to Utilitarianism

1. Ailesbury, *Memoirs* (1890), quoted by J. R. Western, *Monarchy and Revolution: The English State in the 1680s* (London, 1972), p. 98.

2. Thomas Hutchinson, *A Collection of Original Papers Relative to the History of Massachusetts Bay* (Boston, 1769), pp. 199, 170–71.

3. John Davenport, *A Discourse about Civil Government in a New Plantation whose Design is Religion* (Cambridge, Mass., 1663), p. 3.

4. William Hubbard, *The Happiness of a People in the Wisdome of their Rulers Directing and in the Obedience of their Brethren attending Unto what Israel Ought to do* (Boston, 1676), pp. 8–9.

5. Ibid., p. 10. Ecclesiastes 5:15: "As he came forth from his mother's womb, naked shall he go again as he came, and shall take nothing from his labour, which he can carry in his hand." Cf. Job 1:21.

6. Hubbard, *Happiness of a People*, p. 35.

7. Ibid., pp. 54–58. Perry Miller believed that Hubbard spoke for the band of merchants who had come to regard the repeal of the charter as inevitable (*The New England Mind: From Colony to Province* [Cambridge, Mass., 1953], pp. 48–49). If so, Hubbard certainly blasted the spiritual consequences of mercantile activity.

8. Increase Mather, *A Discourse concerning the Danger of Apostasy* (Boston, 1679), which Miller calls "manifestly a rebuttal of Hubbard" (Miller, *New England Mind*, p. 136). See also Mather, *Pray for the Rising Generation* (Boston, 1678), pp. 12, 16.

9. Quoted in Miller, *New England Mind*, p. 28.

10. Ibid., pp. 35–36.

11. Urian Oakes, *New England Pleaded With* (Cambridge, Mass., 1673), pp. 32–33, 18.

12. Increase Mather, *The Day of Trouble is Near* (Cambridge, 1674).

13. Increase Mather, *An Earnest Exhortation to the Inhabitants of New England* (Boston, 1676), p. 11.

14. *The Declaration of the Gentlemen, Merchants, and Inhabitants of Boston, and the Country Adjacent*, (18 April 1689); William Henry Whitmore, ed., *Andros Tracts*, 3 vols. (Boston, 1868–74), 1:14.

15. Miller, *New England Mind*, particularly Book III. The theme has been refined in T. H. Breen's elegant study, *The Character of a Good Ruler: Puritan Political Ideas in New England, 1630–1730* (New Haven, 1970; reprint, New York, 1974), particularly chap. 5. My debt to these works will be apparent to students of the period; I hope, however, to have taken the argument a little further and in slightly different directions.

16. Richard R. Johnson, *Adjustment to Empire: The New England Colonies, 1675–1715* (Leicester, 1981), p. 417, makes what I take to be an essentially similar point when he describes the growth of an increasingly pluralistic and acquisitive society.

17. *The Conditions for New-Planters in the Territories of the Duke of York* ([Boston], 1665). The attribution to Boston is in an inked note in the Library of Congress copy.

18. William Penn, *The Excellent Privilege of Liberty and Property* (Philadelphia, 1687).

19. Thomas Hutchinson, *The History of the Colony and Province of Massachusetts-Bay*, ed. Lawrence Shaw Mayo, 3 vols. (Cambridge, Mass., 1936), 1:302.

20. *The Plain Case Stated . . . to the Prince of Orange* (1689); *An Account of the Late Revolution in New-England in a Letter* (1689); *The Declaration of the Gentlemen, Merchants, and Inhabitants of Boston, and the Country Adjacent* (18 April 1689); Edward Rawson, *The Revolution in New-England Justified* (Boston, 1691); Increase Mather, *A Brief Relation of the State of New-England from the Beginning . . . to 1689* (London, 1689).

21. Increase Mather, *A Vindication of New-England* (Boston, 1690), p. 1.

22. Ibid., p. 26.

23. William Hubbard, *A General History of New England from the Discovery to 1688* (Cambridge, Mass., 1815), pp. 158–59.

24. John Palmer, *An Impartial Account of the State of New England* (London, 1690), pp. 20–21, 38–39.

25. Rawson, *Revolution in New-England Justified*, preface, p. 1.

26. Ibid., p. 42.

27. *Calendar of State Papers Colonial, 1722–1723* (London, 1934), pp. 256–60.

28. Western, *Monarchy and Revolution*, pp. 166–69; Joyce Oldham Appleby, *Economic Thought and Ideology in Seventeenth Century England* (Princeton, 1978), traces this process to the earlier seventeenth century; see esp. chap. 3.

29. Paul Hazard, *La crise de la conscience européenne, 1685–1715* (Paris, 1935), pp. 30–100, 121–57, 245–58; Arthur O. Lovejoy, *The Great Chain of Being* (Baltimore, 1935), pp. 183–207. It was only beginning; I would not argue that these great thinkers were necessarily aware of the consequences, still less that they intended them. Lovejoy, on the contrary, holds that the concept of the Great Chain of Being attained into widest diffusion and acceptance in the eighteenth century. Perhaps, in the true spirit of the owl of Minerva (as Pocock would say), that was because it was reaching the end.

30. J. G. A. Pocock, *The Machiavellian Moment* (Princeton, 1975), chap. 14.

31. Oakes, *New England Pleaded With*; Mather, *An Earnest Exhortation* and *Pray for the Rising Generation*.

32. Cotton Mather, *The Present State of New England* (Boston, 1690), p. 33.

33. Miller, *New England Mind*, p. 162; and note his comment: "That he should have to distinguish, even parenthetically, between a 'will' and an 'ought' was, in 1691, a cloud no bigger than a man's hand on the intellectual horizon."

34. Cotton Mather, *Durable Riches* (Boston, 1695), p. 16.

35. Ibid., pp. 18–19.

36. Ibid., pp. 3–4.

37. Gurdon Saltonstall, *Election Sermon* (Connecticut, 1697), pp. 16, 19.

38. Increase Mather, *The Excellency of a Publick Spirit* (Boston, 1702).

39. Ibid., pp. 3, 13–14, 17–18, 27.

40. Gary M. Nash, *The Urban Crucible: Social Change, Political Consciousness and the Origins of the American Revolution* (Cambridge, Mass., 1979), pp. 61–62, 84–87.

41. Anthony Stoddard, *An Election Sermon* (New London, Conn.,

1716), p. 3; Henry Care, *English Liberties, or the Free-born Subject's Inheritance* (Boston, 1721; reprint, London, 1680?).

42. Thomas Foxcroft, *Observations Historical and Practical on the Rise of New England* (Boston, 1730).

43. Jeremiah Dummer, *A Defence of the New England Charters* (London, 1721).

44. Ibid., pp. 67, 64.

45. Ibid., p. 76.

46. "And shall not the judge of all the earth do right?" (Genesis 18:25). I owe this comment to John Walsh.

47. James Otis, *The Rights of the British Colonies Asserted and proved* (Boston, 1764), in Bernard Bailyn, ed., *Pamphlets of the American Revolution* (Cambridge, Mass., 1965), pp. 419–22.

48. Nash, *Urban Crucible*, pp. 125–28 and chap. 9.

49. *The American Magazine* (Boston, 1743), pp. 1–2.

50. The declining emphasis on religion in government is documented by Lawrence H. Leder, *Liberty and Authority: Early American Political Ideology, 1689–1763* (Chicago, 1968), esp. pp. 51–60, 134–43.

51. Ebenezer Gay, *The Character and Work of a Good Ruler, and the Duty of an Obliged People. An Election Sermon* (Boston, 1745), pp. 4, 5, 16, 18, 22.

52. Candidus [James Chalmers], *Plain Truth* (Philadelphia, 1776), p. 80, quotes this as from "Letter no. 60."

53. Francis Hutcheson, *A Short Introduction to Moral Philosophy* (Glasgow, 1747), Book III, p. 308.

54. *Boston Independent Advertiser*, 8 August 1744, quoted by Leder, *Liberty and Authority*, p. 81.

55. Stanley N. Katz, *Newcastle's New York: Anglo-American Politics, 1732–1753* (Cambridge, Mass., 1968), pp. 74–75; *New-York Weekly Journal*, 11 March 1733/34.

56. *New-York Weekly Journal*, 18 February 1733/34.

57. Nothing is more revealing than the experience of the exiled Thomas Hutchinson, as high a Tory as any man in the colonies. He continued (with some reservations) to support Lord North's administration, but found himself estranged from both the society and the political conduct that lay behind that administration. See Bernard Bailyn, *The Ordeal of Thomas Hutchinson* (Cambridge, Mass., 1974), chap. 8.

58. Bailyn, ed., *Pamphlets*, p. 213. Charles Evans's *Bibliography of Early American Imprints* (New York, 1903–34, reprint 1941) makes no mention even of pamphlets or sermons that may have disappeared.

59. Carl Bridenbaugh, *Mitre and Sceptre: Transatlantic Faiths, Ideas, Personalities, and Politics, 1689–1775* (New York, 1962), records the history of the projected Church of England bishopric and of colonial reactions to it. The point of view is identifiably "Whig" in the American sense.

60. Philopolities [Benjamin Prescott], *A Free and Calm Consideration of the Unhappy Misunderstandings and Debates . . . between the Parliament of Great Britain and these American Colonies by One who was born in Massachusetts-Bay before the reign of William and Mary* (Salem, 1774), p. 20.

61. Bailyn, ed., *Pamphlets*, p. 226. On the charge of plagiarism, pp. 208–9. Bailyn prefers "guilt by association."

62. Jonathan Mayhew, *Discourse Concerning Unlimited Submission*, in Bailyn, ed., *Pamphlets*, p. 221.

63. Milton M. Klein, ed., *The Independent Reflector* (Cambridge, Mass., 1963), p. 287.

64. Ibid., pp. 288, 315–16, 290.

65. Ibid., pp. 306, 312, 315, 319–27.

66. Not that this view of authority had passed without challenge. Students of the period 1629–60 will be well aware that vigorous struggles to extend the basis of representation, to put the laws into fixed and codified form, and to modify the theological basis of the law had left profound marks on the colony's institutions. They had failed, however, to undermine the clergy's claim for the theological sanction of the state, nor had they dissociated the magistracy from that purpose.

67. James Otis, *A Vindication of the Conduct of the House of Representatives of Massachusetts-Bay* (Boston, 1762), pp. 15, 18–19.

68. Thomas R. Adams, *American Independence: The Growth of an Idea* (Providence, R.I., 1965), pp. 37–38. The first letter appeared in the *Pennsylvania Chronicle* on 30 November 1767 and the final one on 8 February 1768. By March they had appeared in pamphlet form.

69. Otis, *Rights of the British Colonies*. His acceptance of this constitutional principle caused acute logical difficulties for the related but not strictly compatible theme that Parliament itself could not set aside

the common law. Otis reiterated the theme of parliamentary supremacy in *A Vindication of the British Colonies* (Boston, 1765).

70. *The Writings of John Dickinson*, ed. Paul Leicester Ford, 2 vols. (Philadelphia, 1895). Cf. Otis, *Rights of the British Colonies*, pp. 426 and 442.

71. *Writings of John Dickinson*, ed. Ford, 1:321.

72. Ibid., p. 401, Letter XII.

73. John Morgan, M.D., F.R.S., *Dissertation on the Reciprocal Advantages of a Perpetual Union between Great Britain and the American Colonies* (Philadelphia, 1766).

74. Ibid, p. 79. Reed may have been the wartime governor of Pennsylvania of the same name; but this seems unlikely because he had long ago finished his formal education and was by this time practicing law in New Jersey. See John F. Roche, *Joseph Reed: A Moderate in the American Revolution* (New York, 1957).

75. Charles M. Andrews, *The Colonial Period of American History* (New Haven, 1938), 4:216; Jack P. Greene, Charles F. Mullett, and Edward C. Papenfuse, Jr., eds., "Magna Charta for America: James Abercromby's 'An Examination of the Acts of Parliament Relative to the Trade and Government of our American Colonies' (1752) and 'De Jure et Gubernatione Colonarium' (1774)," typescript; Leland J. Bellot, *William Knox: The Life and Thought of an Eighteenth Century Imperialist* (Austin, Texas, 1977), pp. 94–98.

76. Grenville in William Cobbett and T. C. Hansard, eds., *The Parliamentary History of England . . . to 1803*, 36 vols. (London, 1806–20), 16:38; Lord Carmarthen was saying the same thing in Parliament as late as 1774. See *Works of the Rt. Hon. Edmund Burke*, ed. Henry Rogers, 2 vols. (London, 1842), 1:174.

77. Bailyn, ed., *Pamphlets*, p. 13; *Works of Burke*, 1:188.

78. Jack P. Greene, "William Knox's Explanation for the American Revolution," *William and Mary Quarterly*, 3d ser., 30 (1973):295.

79. *Works of Burke*, 1:192.

80. *Journals of the Continental Congress*, ed. W. C. Ford, 34 vols. (Washington, D.C., 1904–37), 1:31–37.

81. *Collected Works of Jeremy Bentham*, ed. J. Bowring (Edinburgh, 1838–43), 2:501.

Chapter Two. The Crown in the Colonies

1. Richard L. Morton, *Colonial Virginia*, 2 vols. (Chapel Hill, 1960), 1:172.

2. Thomas Hutchinson, *The History of the Colony and Province of Massachusetts-Bay*, ed. Lawrence Shaw Mayo, 3 vols. (Cambridge, Mass., 1936), 2:2.

3. Michael Garibaldi Hall, *Edward Randolph and the American Colonies, 1676–1703* (1960; reprint, New York, 1969), p. 21.

4. David S. Lovejoy, *The Glorious Revolution in America* (New York, 1972), pp. 22–23, 56–57.

5. For the classical debate see Charles H. McIlwain, *The American Revolution: A Constitutional Interpretation* (New York, 1924); Robert L. Schuyler, *Parliament and the British Empire* (New York, 1929).

6. *The Writings of John Dickinson*, ed. Paul Leicester Ford, 2 vols. (Philadelphia, 1895), 1:312.

7. J. R. Western, *Monarchy and Revolution: The English State in the 1680s* (London, 1972), p. 379.

8. Increase Mather, *A Brief Relation of the State of New England from the Beginning . . . to 1689* (London, 1689), pp. 5, 9.

9. *The Present State of New English Affairs* (broadside) (Boston, 1689).

10. Richard R. Johnson, *Adjustment to Empire: The New England Colonies, 1675–1715* (Leicester, 1981), pp. 142–221, gives a definitively detailed account of these proceedings.

11. Gershom Bulkeley, Esq., *The People's Right to Election, or Alteration of Government in Connecticut, Argued in a Letter* (Philadelphia, 1689).

12. Johnson, *Adjustment to Empire*, pp. 410–11.

13. William Douglass, *A Summary, Historical and Political, of the . . . British Settlements in North-America*, 2 vols. (Boston, 1749, 1751), 2:251.

14. Michael Kammen, *Colonial New York: A History* (New York, 1975), p. 126.

15. *Statutes of the Realm*, 9 Anne C.10.

16. Increase Mather, *The Excellency of a Public Spirit* (Boston, 1702), preface.

17. Ibid., p. 34.

18. Ibid.

19. Ibid., pp. 28–29.

20. Philip S. Haffenden, *New England in the English Nation, 1689–1715* (Oxford, 1974), pp. 59–60. Cotton Mather in 1700 exulted, "It is no little Blessing that we are part of the English Nation" (*Pillar of Gratitude*, cited in ibid.).

21. Ibid., pp. 193–95. But the charter colonies had effective defenders in English political circles.

22. In these cases an act of Parliament would presumably have overcome the legal problems involved in the deprivation of property. What the king had given, Parliament could take away, but only with the monarch's consent.

23. *The Earl of Bellomont's speech to the Assembly 21 March 1698/9* (New York, 1699).

24. *Documents Relative to the Colonial History of the State of New York*, ed. E. B. O'Callaghan (Albany, 1853–87), quoted by Leonard W. Labaree, *Royal Government in America* (New Haven, 1930), p. 382.

25. *Calendar of State Papers Colonial, 1722–1723* (London, 1934), pp. 254–60.

26. Ibid.

27. Ibid., pp. viii, 260.

28. Hutchinson, *History*, 2:178.

29. *Calendar of State Papers Colonial, 1726–1727* (London, 1936), pp. 8–9; see also *Journal of the House of Representatives of Massachusetts*, vol. 6, 1724–26, pp. 458–59. The editor of the *Calendar of State Papers* states inaccurately that the Explanatory Charter was "promulgated to general satisfaction" (1726–27, p. xxix).

30. *Statutes of the Realm*, 6 Geo. 3 C. 12.

31. This statement may not appear to be fully compatible with the fact that bills to restore charters to the crown were five times introduced into Parliament before 1713. James II had proceeded by writs of Quo Warranto but encountered technical difficulties, which had to be overcome by adopting other forms. The legal problem was basically one of property rights; and it is possible that an act of Parliament was considered the best way to deal with these. There is a more fundamental level, however: if Parliament could unmake and make a monarch it could surely unmake a charter. This would be an exercise of that fundamental "legislative power" which had been discovered in the 1640s and which so quickly—if briefly—passed

into the sole keeping of the House of Commons. There seems to have been no suggestion of a parliamentary power to confer a charter, which pertained to the royal prerogative.

32. Elisha Cooke, *Mr. Cooke's Just and Seasonable Vindication* (Boston 1720).

33. "H—," *A Second Letter from one in the Country to his friend in Boston*, 19 March 1728/9.

34. Thomas Prince, *Civil Rulers Raised up by God to feed his People* (Boston, 1728), pp. 21–22.

35. Hutchinson, *History*, 2:260.

36. Ibid., pp. 274–76.

37. Ibid., p. 269.

38. Ibid., p. 284.

39. Douglass, *Summary*, 1:207–8, 210.

40. Loudoun to Halifax, 26 December 1756, Lo 2416, Loudoun Mss., Huntington Library, San Marino, Calif. I am obliged to Paul Langford for this reference. Loudoun, who quarreled violently with the colonists, can hardly be considered a disinterested witness. His controversy with Governor Thomas Pownall in Massachusetts was soon generalized into a clash with the General Court, which passed a law to permit quartering of troops in public buildings but not in private houses. Pownall, who condemned Loudoun's methods as aggressive and unconstitutional, perceived that he was alienating Americans from the British Empire. See Alan Rogers, *Empire and Liberty: American Resistance to British Authority, 1755–1763* (Berkeley, 1974), pp. 84–86.

Chapter Three. The Challenge of Parliament

1. Jennifer Carter, "The Revolution and the Constitution," in Geoffrey Holmes, ed., *Britain after the Glorious Revolution, 1689–1714* (London, 1969), p. 39.

2. J. R. Western, *Monarchy and Revolution: The English State in the 1680s* (London, 1972), p. 28. Cumberland believed that social happiness arose from individual happiness but that even the satisfaction of brutal appetites could promote the public good.

3. *New York Weekly Journal*, 12 November 1733.

4. Western, *Monarchy and Revolution*, pp. 386–87: "England was a real monarchy, not a crowned republic."

5. Carter, "The Revolution and the Constitution," p. 52.

6. Charles M. Andrews, *The Colonial Period of American History*, 4 vols. (New Haven, 1938), 4:389–91.

7. Western, *Monarchy and Revolution*, p. 351.

8. Ibid., p. 312.

9. P. G. M. Dickson, *The Financial Revolution in England* (London, 1967), pp. 13, 203.

10. Geoffrey Holmes, *British Politics in the Age of Anne* (London, 1967), p. 382.

11. Richard R. Johnson, *Adjustment to Empire: The New England Colonies, 1675–1715* (Leicester, 1981), p. 276.

12. J. R. Pole, *Political Representation in England and the Origins of the American Republic* (New York, 1966; reprint, 1971), p. 129; Jack P. Greene, *The Quest for Power: The Lower Houses of Assembly in the Southern Royal Provinces, 1689–1776* (Chapel Hill, 1963), passim.

13. P. D. G. Thomas, *The House of Commons in the Eighteenth Century* (Oxford, 1971), p. 104.

14. Leonard W. Labaree, *Royal Government in America* (New Haven, 1930), p. 304.

15. Norman Baker, "Changing Attitudes towards Government in Eighteenth Century Britain," in Anne Whiteman, J. S. Bromley, and P. G. M. Dickson, *Statesmen, Scholars and Merchants: Essays in Eighteenth Century History Presented to Dame Lucy Sutherland* (Oxford, 1973), p. 204.

16. *Calendar of State Papers Colonial, 1726–1727* (London, 1936), p. 50.

17. Andrews, *Colonial Period*, 4:407.

18. Thomas Hutchinson, *The History of the Colony and Province of Massachusetts-Bay*, ed. Lawrence Mayo Shaw, 3 vols. (Cambridge, Mass., 1936), 2:301.

19. Joseph Albert Ernst, *Money and Politics in America, 1755–1775* (Chapel Hill, 1973), pp. 30–31.

20. Hutchinson, *History*, 2:301.

21. *The American Magazine* (Boston, 1744), pp. 243–44.

22. William Douglass, *A Discourse concerning the Currencies of the*

British Plantations in America (Boston, 1740), p. 21. Evans attributed this work to Hutchinson.

23. Ibid., pp. 41, 45.

24. *American Magazine,* pp. 281–86, 306–7.

25. *An Account of the Rise, Progress, and Consequences of the Land Bank; and the Silver Schemes* (Boston, 1744), pp. 39–40.

26. Ibid., pp. 46–47.

27. *Boston Gazette,* 1–8 December 1740, 5–12 January 1741.

28. *Boston Weekly News-Letter,* 1–9 April 1742.

29. Loudoun Mss., Lo 6281, Huntington Library. I am again indebted to Paul Langford.

30. Hutchinson, *History,* 3:48.

31. James Otis, *A Vindication of the Conduct of House of Representatives of Massachusetts-Bay* (Boston, 1762).

32. Ibid., p. 52. This position needs to be compared with Otis's apparent surrender to parliamentary power in 1764 in *The Rights of the British Colonies Asserted and Proved* (Bernard Bailyn, ed., *Pamphlets of the American Revolution* [Cambridge, Mass., 1965], p. 442). The change in position reflected the ambiguities and unresolved difficulties already mentioned—not to mention the sheer fact of parliamentary power as demonstrated on the rare occasions when Parliament had unsheathed it.

33. Archibald Kennedy, *Observations on the Importance of the Northern Colonies under Proper Regulations* (New York, 1750), p. 4; Benjamin Franklin, *Observations on the Increase of Mankind* (Philadelphia, 1755), in Leonard W. Labaree, ed., *The Papers of Benjamin Franklin,* 14 vols. (New Haven, 1959–61), 4:228. And compare Stuart Bruchey, *The Roots of American Economic Growth, 1607–1861: An Essay in Social Causation* (New York, 1968), pp. 18–21.

34. Jack P. Greene, Charles F. Mullett, and Edward C. Papenfuse, Jr., eds., "Magna Charta for America: James Abercromby's 'An Examination of the Act of Parliament Relative to the Trade and Government of our American Colonies,'" typescript, p. 261.

35. Ibid., p. 61.

36. Ibid., p. 65.

37. Greene et al., eds., "De Jure et Gubernatione Coloniarum" in ibid., p. 334. By 1774, however, Abercromby was confronting a

changed situation, and he then attacked notions of divided sovereignty as not only "derogatory in common sense, but totally inconsistent with our Constitution" (ibid., p. 289).

38. Alan Rogers, *Empire and Liberty: American Resistance to British Authority, 1755–1763* (Berkeley, 1974), pp. 13–16, 76–78.

39. *Journal of the House of Representatives* (Boston, 1764), pp. 53, 66, 72–77.

40. Reprinted in *Boston Post-Boy and Advertiser*, 15 July 1765.

41. [William Hicks], *The Nature and Extent of Parliamentary Power Considered* (reprinted from the *Pennsylvania Journal*, New York, 1768), p. 5. The author appears to have been the William Hicks who was a member of the Pennsylvania council from September 1771. This attribution is made in the two Library of Congress copies. He is not in *Dictionary of American Biography*.

42. Philopolites [Benjamin Prescott], *A Free and Calm Consideration of the Unhappy Misunderstandings and Debates . . . between the Parliament of Great Britain and these American Colonies by One who was born in Massachusetts-Bay before the reign of William and Mary* (Salem, 1774), p. 11.

43. Ibid., pp. 42–43.

44. *The Works of James Wilson*, ed. Robert Green McCloskey, 2 vols. (Cambridge, Mass., 1967), 2:721–46.

45. *The Papers of Thomas Jefferson*, ed. Julian P. Boyd et al., 19 vols. (Princeton, 1950–71), 1:121–37.

46. Merrill Jensen, *The Founding of a Nation: A History of the American Revolution, 1763–1776* (New York, 1968), pp. 334–35.

47. William Blackstone, *Commentaries on the Laws of England*, 4 vols. (London, 1876), 1:21.

48. Jack P. Greene, "William Knox's Explanation for the American Revolution," *William and Mary Quarterly*, 3d ser., 30 (1973):293–306.

49. This is a theme which I hope to explore in future. For a preliminary attempt, see J. R. Pole, "Enlightenment and the Politics of American Nature," in Roy Porter and Mikulas Teich, eds., *The Enlightenment in National Context* (Cambridge, 1981), pp. 210–11.

50. *Works of James Wilson*, 2:723–24. Well-known now but probably not very widely read at the time, it was printed only once. See Thomas R. Adams, *American Independence: The Growth of an Idea* (Providence, 1965), p. xii. [John Allen], "British Bostonian," in *The American Alarm*

(Boston, 1773), reached a similar conclusion. Allen accepted the governor's thesis that no line could be drawn between the supreme authority of Parliament and the total independence of the colonies but denied such parliamentary power. British Americans were the equals of those at home, hence had the same rights, and American parliaments were therefore supreme in the colonies (pp. 2–3).

51. *Works of James Wilson*, 2:741.

Chapter Four. The Problem of Communication

1. This process is traced in J. R. Pole, *Political Representation in England and the Origins of the American Republic* (London and New York, 1966; reprint, Berkeley, 1971), pp. 442–57, 494–99, 526; it is missed in John Cannon, *Parliamentary Reform* (Cambridge, 1973).

2. F. W. Maitland, *The Constitutional History of England* (Cambridge, 1919), pp. 241–42.

3. Hooker [John Vowell], *The Order and Usage of Keeping a Parlement* (1575), pp. 25, 28, 32–33.

4. J. E. Neale, *The Elizabethan House of Commons* (London, 1949), p. 417.

5. Sir Simonds D'Ewes, *The Journal of all the Parliaments during the Reign of Queen Elizabeth* (London, 1682), p. 433.

6. Neale, *Elizabethan House of Commons*, pp. 389, 417.

7. Ibid., pp. 417–18.

8. Maitland, *Constitutional History of England*, pp. 247–48.

9. *House of Commons Journal*, 1:118–19 (hereinafter *CJ*).

10. Ibid., pp. 333–36.

11. Ibid., pp. 55, 73, 86. The unusual character of divisions is suggested in 1558 by the journal's cumbrous and seemingly inexperienced description of the procedure.

12. Ibid., pp. 878, 896.

13. Ibid., pp. 893–94.

14. Wallace Notestein, *The Winning of the Initiative by the House of Commons* (London, 1924).

15. Derek Hirst, *The Representative of the People?* (Cambridge, 1975), p. 161.

16. Ibid., pp. 178–81.

17. Ibid., p. 182.

18. P. W. Thomas, *Sir John Berkenhead, 1617–1679* (Oxford, 1969), p. 28.

19. *CJ*, 2:84.

20. Ibid., p. 26.

21. Ibid., pp. 166, 588, 624, 719, 736.

22. *An Ordinance of the Lords and Commons in Parliament assembled* . . . 28 September 1647, AA.1.19.(105), Library of Worcester College, Oxford.

23. *CJ*, 8:417–18, 435.

24. *Master Pym's Speech in Parliament*, BB.1.16.(99), Worcester College. Pym here described Parliament as "the supreme council." See also Thomas May, *The History of the Parliament of England, which began November the Third, MDCXL* (London, 1647), p. 60.

25. *The Diurnal Occurrences of every dayes proceeding in PARLIAMENT.* . . . (London, 1641), BB.1.16.(1), Worcester College.

26. Margaret Atwood Judson, "Henry Parker and the Theory of Parliamentary Sovereignty," in *Essays in History and Political Theory in Honor of Charles Howard McIlwain* (Cambridge, Mass., 1936), pp. 138–67; J. R. Pole, *The Seventeenth Century: The Sources of Legislative Power* (Charlottesville, Va., 1969), pp. 9–11.

27. Neale, *Elizabethan House of Commons*, p. 397.

28. W. H. Coates, ed., *The Journal of Sir Simonds D'Ewes* (New Haven, 1942), p. xxvii.

29. Ibid., pp. 106, 183–86, 294–95.

30. May, *History of Parliament*, pp. 85–86.

31. Ibid., pp. 113–14.

32. Clarke Papers, Worcester College, Oxford, Mss. 40, 42, 44, 62. See Barbara Taft, "Voting Lists of the Council of Officers, December, 1648," *Bulletin of the Institute of Historical Research* 52, no. 126 (1979):138–54.

33. D'Ewes, *Journal*, p. 165.

34. *Works of the Rt. Hon. Edmund Burke*, ed. Henry Rogers, 2 vols. (London, 1842), 1:180.

35. *Freeholders Journal*, 7 March 1721; John Perceval, Earl of Egmont, *Faction Detected by the Evidence of Facts, Containing an Impartial View of Parties at Home, and Affairs Abroad* (London, 1743), p. 101.

36. D'Ewes, *Journal*, p. 165.

37. Peter Fraser, *The Intelligence of the Secretaries of State, 1660–1688* (Cambridge, 1956), p. 124.

38. H. M. Margiliouth, ed., *The Poems and Letters of Andrew Marvell*, 2 vols. (Oxford, 1971) 2:7, 25, 50, 51, 52.

39. William Cobbett and T. C. Hansard, eds., *The Parliamentary History of England . . . to 1803*, 36 vols. (London, 1806–20), 5:166 (hereinafter *Parl. Hist.*). Joyce O. Appleby, *Economic Thought and Ideology in Seventeenth-Century England* (Princeton, 1978), pp. 209–40.

40. Sheila Lambert, "Printing for the House of Commons in the Eighteenth Century," *The Library*, 5th ser., 23 (1968):25–46.

41. *CJ*, 11:193.

42. Lambert, "Printing for the House of Commons." For the first three days of the session a higher charge was made at four and a half pence for the *Votes*. The Speaker made a profit on these transactions, which took place under his authority.

43. C. S. Emden, *People and the Constitution* (Oxford, 1956), pp. 119–20.

44. Geoffrey Holmes, *The Electorate and the National Will in the First Age of Party* (Lancaster, 1976), p. 7.

45. *Hansard's Parliamentary Debates*, 3d ser., 21 (London, 1834): 239–45.

46. Aubrey Newman, ed., *The Parliamentary Lists of the Early Eighteenth Century: Their Compilation and Use* (Leicester, 1973), pp. 15, 22.

47. Ibid., p. 26. Newman notes occasional deliberate errors in the ascription of names (p. 15), which testifies to the propagandist character of the lists but not to their accuracy as record. See also Romney Sedgwick, *The House of Commons, 1715–1754* (London, 1970), pp. 126–31.

48. Charles M. Andrews, *The Colonial Period of American History*, 4 vols. (New Haven, 1938), 4:358 and n. 2.

49. *Freeholders Journal*, 7 March 1722.

50. *Weekly Journal and Saturday Post*, 24 March 1722.

51. Newman, ed., *Parliamentary Lists*, pp. 36–37.

52. Sedgwick, *House of Commons*, p. 16.

53. Bonamy Dobrée, ed., *The Letters of Lord Chesterfield*, 2 vols. (London, 1932), 2:400–402.

54. Sir Lewis Namier and John Brooke, *The House of Commons, 1754–1790* (London, 1964), p. 530.

55. P. D. G. Thomas, *The House of Commons in the Eighteenth Century* (Oxford, 1971), pp. 68–69.

56. *Parl. Hist.*, 10:800–812.

57. Ibid., p. 812.

58. Benjamin Beard Hoover, *Samuel Johnson's Parliamentary Reporting: Debates in the Senate of Lilliput* (Berkeley, 1953), pp. 6, 11, 23–24, 33.

59. Ibid., p. 33. Johnson, however, regarded the speeches he composed as a literary exercise and did not expect readers to take them literally. He was mortified when he learned that some had done so and even on his deathbed regretted the implied deception.

60. John Almon, *Memoirs of John Almon, Bookseller of Piccadilly* (London, 1790), p. 119; P. D. G. Thomas, "The Beginning of Parliamentary Reporting in the Newspapers, 1768–1774," *English Historical Review* 74 (1959): 626.

61. Sir Henry Cavendish, *Debates in the House of Commons* (London, 1840), pp. 256–60, 312–13, 377.

62. *Parl. Hist.*, 17:68–69.

63. *Works of Burke*, 1:148. Burke is reported as saying that he had "frequently seen reports of my speeches directly contrary to the sentiments I had uttered." This would only increase the odium. "So long as they feel an interest in examining into the proceedings in Parliament, so long you will find a man that will print them" (Cavendish, *Debates*, pp. 259–60). Short of complete suppression, which, as Burke argued, was impossible in the long run, the only corrective to these abuses was accurate reporting. The force of this argument made itself felt gradually but effectively.

64. Almon, *Memoirs*, p. 120, gives an account of these well-known events from memory. They constitute perhaps the only part of our story that takes its place in conventional histories.

65. *Parl. Hist.*, 17:122–63.

66. Thomas, *House of Commons*, p. 145.

67. Ibid., pp. 34, 143.

68. Ibid., p. 147.

69. Robert L. Haig, *The Gazetteer, 1735–1797* (Carbondale, Ill., 1960), pp. 190–93.

70. Josef Redlich, *The Procedure of the House of Commons*, 2 vols. (London, 1908), p. 38.

71. John Hatsell, *Precedents of Proceedings in the House of Commons*, 2 vols. (1818; reprint, Shannon, 1971), 2:180.

72. Ibid.

73. Ibid., p. 181.

74. Thomas, *House of Commons*, pp. 139, 142.

75. Ibid., p. 142.

76. Ibid., p. 148.

77. Redlich, *Procedure*, 2:35.

Chapter Five. Telling the American People

1. Stephen Saunders Webb, *The Governors-General: The English Army and the Definition of the Empire, 1569–1681* (Chapel Hill, 1979), pp. 287, 367–68, 406–8, 459.

2. *Archives of Maryland*, ed. W. H. Browne, 65 vols. (Baltimore, 1883–1952), 2:41, 329.

3. Webb, *Governors-General*, p. 406; John C. Rainbolt, "The Alteration in the Relationship between Leadership and Constituents in Virginia, 1660–1720," *William and Mary Quarterly*, 3d ser., 27 (1970): 411–34; *Journals of the House of Burgesses*, ed. Henry Read McIlwaine (Richmond, 1905–15), 1659/60–1693, pp. 167–68.

4. *Journals of the House of Burgesses*, 2:201, 210.

5. Susan Rosenfeld Falb, "Proxy Voting in Early Maryland Assemblies," *Maryland Historical Magazine* 73 (1978): 217–18; *Archives of Maryland*, 1:6–7.

6. *Archives of Maryland*, 1:93.

7. Ibid., 1:261–62.

8. *Journals of the House of Burgesses*, 2:135.

9. Mary P. Clarke, *Parliamentary Privilege in the American Colonies* (New Haven, 1943), p. 126.

10. *Journal of the House of Representatives of Massachusetts*, 6:427, 458–59.

11. *Boston News-Letter*, 9–16 December 1725, 13–20 January 1726; *New-England Courant*, 15–22 January 1726.

12. *Pennsylvania Archives*, 8th ser., 8 vols. (Harrisburg, 1935), 5:3690, 3701.

13. *Massachusetts House Journal*, 17:260, 261; 18:47–48.

14. Thomas Hutchinson *History of the Colony and Province of*

Massachusetts-Bay, ed. Lawrence Shaw Mayo, 3 vols. (Cambridge, Mass., 1936), 2:260–61.

15. Americanus, *A Letter to the Freeholders* (broadside) (1739).

16. Cinncinatus, L. Quincius, *A Letter to the Freeholders* (Boston, 1749).

17. William Douglass, *A Summary, Historical and Political, of the . . . British Settlements in North-America,* 2 vols. (Boston, 1749, 1751), 2:491.

18. Thomas Thumb, *The Monster of Monsters* (Boston, 1754); Daniel Fowle, *A Total Eclipse of Liberty* (Boston, 1755); *Appendix* to the above (1756); *Massachusetts House Journal,* 31:63.

19. *Archives of Maryland,* 24:679; Daniel Dulany, *The Right of the Inhabitants of Maryland to the Benefit of the English Laws* (Annapolis, 1728); *The Charter of Maryland together with the Debates and Proceedings of the Upper and Lower Houses of Assembly in the Years 1722, 1723 and 1724* (Philadelphia, 1725); St. G. L. Sioussat, *Economics and Politics in Maryland, 1720–1750* (Baltimore, 1903).

20. Aubrey C. Land, *The Dulanys of Maryland* (Baltimore, 1955), p. 68.

21. *Archives of Maryland,* 37:447.

22. Land, *Dulanys of Maryland,* p. 23.

23. *Archives of Maryland,* 59:26–27, 151–52, 159, 161–62, 164.

24. *Journals of the House of Assembly of Jamaica, 1733–1734* (1811–16), pp. 232–33 .

25. Patricia U. Bonomi, *A Factious People: Politics and Society in Colonial New York* (New York, 1971), pp. 135–36. But a division list had already been printed by Zenger in 1733, presumably as part of his proprietor's general posture of challenge to authority (*New York Weekly Journal,* December 1733). For further recorded divisions, see *Journal of Votes and Proceedings of the General Assembly of New York, 1737* (New York, 1764), pp. 711, 712, 716–17, 724.

26. A. R. Hasse, "The First Published Proceedings of an American Legislature," reprinted from *A Journal of the House of Representatives for His Majesty's Province of New York,* in *New York Public Library Bulletin,* February–April 1903. I am indebted to Jack P. Greene for this reference.

27. Leonard W. Levy, *Legacy of Suppression* (Cambridge, Mass., 1960), pp. 44–46; *Journal, General Assembly of New York,* 2:65, 173, 192–93, 198.

28. Levy, *Legacy of Suppression*, p. 45.

29. Leonard W. Labaree, ed., *The Papers of Benjamin Franklin*, 14 vols. (New Haven, 1959–62), 5:529–31.

30. *Pennsylvania Archives*, 8th ser., 5:4245–50.

31. Ibid., 8:7019, 6962, 6985.

32. *Boston Gazette and Country Journal*, 31 March 1766; *Boston Evening-Post* (supplement), 28 April 1766; Merrill Jensen, ed., *English Historical Documents*, 9 (London, 1955):732–36.

33. *Boston Gazette*, 2 June 1766; *Massachusetts Gazette Extraordinary*, 29 May 1766; *Boston Evening-Post*, 2 June 1766.

34. *Pennsylvania Gazette*, 2 May 1765.

35. James Otis, *A Vindication of the Conduct of the House of Representatives of Massachusetts-Bay* (Boston, 1762).

36. *Boston Gazette*, 31 March 1766.

37. Ibid., 5 May 1766.

38. Bernard Mason, ed., *The American Colonial Crisis: The Daniel Leonard–John Adams Letters to the Press, 1774–1775* (New York, 1972), pp. 15, 152–53.

39. *Boston Gazette*, 2 June 1766.

40. Ibid., 12 June 1766; *Journals of the House of Burgesses*, 1764, 2 November.

41. Gordon S. Wood, *The Creation of the American Republic, 1776–1787* (Chapel Hill, 1969), esp. pp. 600–602. His point is that the rulers and the ruled became coextensive in the new American political science.

42. Francis Newton Thorpe, ed., *The Federal and State Constitutions, Colonial Charters, and Other Organic Laws*, 7 vols. (Washington, D.C., 1909), pp. 15, 21, 540, 571, 793, 988–89, 1061, 1722–23, 1894, 2426, 2902, 3272, 2632, 2794, 3085, 3839; Luther Stearns Cushing, *Elements of the Law and Practice of Legislative Assemblies of the United States of America* (Boston, 1856), pp. 138–42. Cushing implies that the requirement of the state legislatures for information of the proceedings of their delegations in the Continental Congress appeared to have prompted the practice of recording individual votes in assembly journals. A touch of skepticism about this opinion was my own point of departure for this inquiry into the history of the recording and reporting of legislative divisions and, subsequently, debates (ibid., pp. 164–65).

43. *Pennsylvania Gazette,* 21 September 1774; Lester Cappon, ed., *Adams-Jefferson Letters,* 2 vols. (Chapel Hill, 1959), 1:4; Jack N. Rakove, *The Beginnings of National Politics* (New York, 1979), p. 248.

44. Cushing, *Elements of the Law,* p. 165; Rakove, *Beginnings of National Politics,* pp. 128–32, 268–74; *Journals of the Continental Congress,* ed. W. C. Ford, 34 vols. (Washington, D.C., 1904–37), 8:676–77. Congress had recently begun to record the yeas and nays at the request of states.

45. Cecelia M. Kenyon, ed., *The Antifederalists* (Indianapolis, 1966); Jackson Turner Main, *The Antifederalists: Critics of the Constitution, 1781–1788* (Chapel Hill, 1961).

46. Paul Langford, "British Correspondence in the Colonial Press, 1763–1775: A Study in Anglo-American Misunderstanding before the American Revolution," in Bernard Bailyn and John B. Hench, eds., *The Press and the American Revolution* (Worcester, Mass., 1980), pp. 279–309.

47. William V. Wells, ed., *The Life and Public Services of Samuel Adams,* 3 vols. (Boston, 1865), 1:240–42, laments the silence of the colonial newspapers in matters of legislative reporting, but this is the only specific comment that I can recall.

48. P. D. G. Thomas, *The House of Commons in the Eighteenth Century* (Oxford, 1971), p. 200.

49. *Pennsylvania Evening Herald,* 9 November 1785.

50. Mathew Carey, ed., *Debates and Proceedings of the General Assembly of Pennsylvania on . . . the Charter of the Bank* (Philadelphia, 1788).

51. *New York Journal,* 25 January 1787; *New York Packet,* 6 February 1786 (reporting a debate in the Pennsylvania Assembly); *Middlesex Gazette* (Connecticut), 19 June 1786 (giving a sarcastic account of the session), 21 August 1786, 23 October 1786; *American Herald,* 16 October 1786; *Pennsylvania Gazette,* 1 November 1786, 22, 29 November 1786. Congressional privacy also gave way: on 2 May 1786 the *Daily Advertiser* (New York) reported a division list in Congress, with internal breakdown by states.

52. *New York Journal,* 18 January 1787.

53. *Gazette of the United States,* "Published at the Seat of Government beginning April 14, 1790," New York, then Philadelphia. *The National Gazette,* 7 November 1791, begins with a report on the House

debate on the number of representatives to be allocated to each district.

54. *Annals of the Congress of the United States*, comp. Joseph Gales, Sr. (Washington, D.C., 1834), 3d Cong., 1st sess., 1:42, 43, 44. The practice of calling for a division spread gradually and was evidently rare at this time in Virginia, where the *Gazette of the United States* commented on a defeated bill to make land subject to execution in debt settlements that the minority, "by calling for the yeas and nays, have disclosed to their constituents those who were adverse to the measure" (27 November 1795).

55. *Annals of Congress*, 3d Cong., 1st sess., 1:45.

56. Ibid., 1st Cong., 2d sess., 1:1059–61.

57. Ibid., *House Journal*, 2:735–37.

58. *Washington Federalist*, 13 January 1802.

Chapter Six. Government and Happiness

1. J. G. A. Pocock, "The Revolution against Parliament," in J. G. A. Pocock, ed., *Three British Revolutions* (Princeton, 1980), p. 285.

2. Lawrence Stone, "The Results of the English Revolutions," in ibid., p. 80.

3. *Encyclopaedia Brittanica* (Edinburgh, 1771), vol. 2.

4. For which reason I think that Joyce Appleby writes of "the pursuit of happiness" as "Jefferson's tellingly modern phrase" at some risk of misunderstanding. It did not even sound particularly modern in 1776. As she has pointed out to me, however, the emphasis falls on "pursuit," rather than on "happiness," and in this sense she has history on her side.

Index

Abbot, Speaker Charles, 114
Abercromby, James, 37, 80–81, 85
Adams, John, 130, 131
Adams, Samuel, 128, 130
Adams, Samuel, Sr., 78
Albany Conference, 81
Allen, James, 123
Allen, John, 164–65 (n. 50)
Almon, John, 111
America: social change in, 4;
common interest with England,
13; characteristics of, 21, 47;
ideology and public opinion, 28,
30, 31, 35, 37, 65–66, 83, 84, 137,
145–46, 161 (n. 40); disorders in,
33; self-government by, 41
The American Magazine, 24
American Revolution, 9–10, 15–16,
39, 47, 79–80, 143; sentiment of,
anticipated, 56; and internal
changes, 131, 140; concept of
happiness in, 147
"Americanus" [pseud. for a
pamphleteer], 122
Andros, Governor Sir Edmund, 6,
9–12, 14, 18, 48, 61, 79; his regime
held illegal, 144
Anglicans: in New England, 18, 29,
30
Anne, Queen of England, 47; death
of, 54, 68, 69; wars of, 70;
Parliament under, 72; party
warfare under, 142
Appleby, Joyce: takes
unprecedented risk, 173 (n. 4)

Arminianism: of Mayhew, 30; of
Church of England, 32. *See also*
Church of England
Army council: Putney Debates, 101
Articles of Confederation:
ratification delayed, 132
Assemblies, colonial, 52, 56, 65–66,
84–85, 87, 89, 142; aligned with
governors, 33; "rise of," 72, 143;
and legitimacy, 102; journals of,
117–18, 119; communication with
public, 126–30, 135–36
Authority, political: sources of, 1

Bacon, Sir Francis, 94
Bacon's Rebellion, 33, 117–18
Bailyn, Bernard, 38
Baltimore, Lord, Proprietor of
Maryland, 124
Bank of England, 68
Bank of North America, 137
Baptists, 24
Barbados, 14
Belcher, Governor Jonathan, 62, 122
Bellomont, Governor the Earl of,
54–55
Benevolence: as philosophical
principle, 25–26, 67, 147
Bentham, Jeremy, 40
Berkeley, Governor William, 42
Bernard, Governor Francis, 33–34,
62, 83, 128
Beverley, Robert, 117–18
Bible, 4
Blackstone, Sir William: author of

Index

Index

10, 14, 22, 23, 42; social thought in, 32; mutual value of British connection, 36; too much "democratic power" in, 38–39; charters, 42, 49, 68; and British government, 46, 52, 56, 61, 69–70, 72, 80, 145; character of, 63, 81; stable governments in, 143; ideological consistency among, 144

Commerce, 22, 23, 36, 54, 144

Common law, 32, 157–58 (n. 69)

Commonwealth, 3, 6, 43

"Commonwealthsman," 14, 30

Communication, xiii, 87–90

Congregationalism: in New England, 29, 30; ministers of, 2, 9, 11. *See also* Clergy

Congress, Continental, xiv, 40, 84, 132; secrecy of, 131, 132; as new representative institution, 145; adopts Jefferson's language, 146; records yeas and nays, 172 (n. 44)

Congress, U.S., xiv, 139

Connecticut, 123; election sermon by Stoddard, 21; Bulkeley on government of, 50–51; charter, 51; escapes Act of Toleration, 59; disaffection toward Britain, 63; assembly debates reported, 137

Consent: James Wilson on, 86; becomes active principle, 131

Constitution, British, 61, 62, 66, 71, 84, 85; army debates and, 101–2

Constitution, U.S., 134

Constitutional Convention (1787), 133–34

Constitutional ideas: British and American, xiii

Constitutions: of states, 131

Contract: as metaphor, 40; linked to charters, 60

Conway, Henry, 113

Cooke, Elisha, Jr., 59–60, 62

Cooke, Elisha, Sr., 15

Cosby, Governor William, 27, 125

Council: in colonial government, 16, 70

Council of Trade and Plantations, 58

"A Countryman" [pseud. for a letter writer], 129

Country party: in Massachusetts, 15, 16, 62; in Britain, 69, 103; purer in colonies, 69

Court: as element in colonial politics, 28, 122; in British politics, 103

The Craftsman, 108

Cromwell, Oliver, 65, 143

Crosby, Brass, Lord Mayor of London, 112

Crown: of England, 1, 5, 10, 44; and colonies, 16, 22, 33, 45, 50–51, 53–56, 59–61, 83, 143; and national defense, 34; source of charters, 42, 49, 51; Shute's claims exceed, 57; and contract theory, 60; and Parliament, 67–68, 90, 100; prerogative, 93, 95; bills to restore colonies to, 160 (n. 31). *See also* Monarchy

Culpeper, Governor Lord, 118

Cumberland, Richard, 67, 161 (n. 2)

Cushing, Luther Stearns: on origin of recording assembly divisions, 171 (n. 42)

The Daily Gazetteer, 113

Davenport, John, 7

Deane, Silas, 132

Debates, legislative: not reported by colonial press, 134; silence of, a loss to historians, 135, 172 (n. 47); Carey reports, 136–37, 149–50

Declaratory Act, 35, 39, 45, 54

Democracy: absent from earlier theory, 15, 25; modern, 88; theory of, 89; under Triennial Act, 144

Descartes, René, 18

Index

Index

The Gentleman's Magazine, 109

George I, King of England, 54, 106; his death desired, 56; Cooke's loyalty to, 60

George III, King of England, 18; views presumed in Massachusetts, 34; allegiance to, renounced by colonies, 46

Georgia: origins of, 42

Glorious Revolution, 3, 18, 31, 40; in New England, 12–14, 45, 61; in colonial opinion, 46–48, 64; in English opinion, 47, 61; and happiness, 60; Settlement, 66

God, xiii, 6, 9, 17, 18, 21, 26; intentions of, 7–8; quarrels with Massachusetts, 8; loves losers, 19; made William III king of England, 52; character of, transformed by philosophers, 67

Goldthwait, Thomas, 129

Gordon, Thomas: as "Cato," 26

Government, xiii; obligations of, 2, 4–6, 9, 15, 17, 20–21, 24, 25, 28, 31–33, 146–48; civil, 7; popular in New England, 14; right to self-government questioned, 15

Governors: of colonies, 15, 22, 33, 51, 57–59, 61–62, 69, 118. *See also individual governors*

Grand Memorandum, 105

Grand Remonstrance, 100–101, 102, 104

Great Awakening, 24

Great Chain of Being, 7

Greenwich, Manor of, 13

Halifax, Earl of, 63

Halifax, Marquis of, 71

Hamilton, Alexander, 138

Hampden, John, 65

Hanover, House of, 28, 54

Happiness, 7, 20, 38, 141–48; government's obligation to, 31, 32, 33, 40; of New York due to royal government, 54; and Hanoverian monarchs, 60; James Wilson on, 86; whether pursuit of, "modern" in 1776, 173 (n. 4)

Hatsell, John, 114

Headlam, Cecil, 56

Hicks, William, 83, 164 (n. 41)

High Commission, Court of, 6

Hirst, Derek, 97

History, 89; recent research in colonial American, xiv–xv; a question of, 47; American view of English, 65

Hobby, Sir Edward, 91–92

Holmes, Geoffrey, 106

Hooker. *See* Vowell, John

House of Commons, 43, 57, 65, 69, 70, 90–91, 124; privacy of, 90–93, 95–96, 113; establishes censorship, 98–99; enlists public support, 99; in 1641, 102; publishes *Votes,* 104–5; its *Journal,* 105; divisions in, 107; public access to, 113–16; minority arguments in, replicated in Boston, 130; as theater, 136; represents new interests, 144. *See also* Parliament

House of Lords, 88, 102, 103, 104. *See also* Parliament

House of Representatives, 139–40

Howe brothers, 113

Hubbard, William, 7, 8, 13, 17

Hutcheson, Francis, 27

Hutchinson, Thomas: governor and historian, 11, 21, 76, 78–79; dispute with General Court, 84; in exile, 156 (n. 57)

Independence: rumors of, in Massachusetts, 22; Massachusetts denied, 23, 62; sentiment in early New York, 54

The Independent Reflector, 31

Indians, 56

Index

Individualism, 19
Instruction: of representatives, 97; Burke confutes doctrine of, 103; as in Holland, 104; on Place Bill, 108; for colonial rights, 127
Interests: private, as colonial motive, 5, 8, 11, 13, 16, 21, 36, 87, 88; clergy worried by, 18, 20; in Parliament, 88, 144
"Intolerable Acts," 45
Ireland: considered as conquered province, 12, 14
Italy: source of humanist thought, 18

Jamaica, 14, 74; move to introduce Poyning's law into, 44; journals of, House of Representatives, 118, 125
James II, King of England, 6, 10, 28, 49, 73, 106; proceeds against Massachusetts charter, 45; proceeding against Connecticut charter, 51; overthrown, 65; proceedings against New England charters, 160 (n. 31)
Jefferson, Thomas, 18; author of *Summary View of Rights of British America*, 84; complains about lack of information from Congress, 131; drafts Declaration of Independence, 146; concept of happiness, 147; on pursuit of happiness, 173 (n. 4)
Johnson, Samuel: his parliamentary reporting, 110, 168 (n. 59); defines happiness, 147

King: of England. *See* Crown, Monarchy
Knox, William, 37, 38, 85

Land Bank: Massachusetts, 26, 75, 76, 78; debates on, not reported, 135

Laud, William, Archbishop of Canterbury, 13, 98
Law: its role in social order, 32; Blackstone on "will," 85; Maryland claims equal rights in, 124
Lee, Arthur, 132
Legislative power, 22
Legislatures. *See* Assemblies, House of Commons, House of Lords, Parliament, Representation
Legitimacy, 86, 102; through election, 103; through public knowledge, 140
Leibnitz, G. W., 18
Leisler, Jacob, 51
Leonard, Daniel: as "Massachusettensis," 130
Liberty, 20, 22, 31, 65; civil and religious, restored by Parliament, 52–53; menaced by government, 148
Licensing Act, 27, 99
Livingston, William, 30–31, 32
Locke, John, 18, 31; as authority for American revolt, 46; cited by Otis, 80
London, 22, 49, 50, 112; newsletters, 105; newspapers, 111; its magnetism, 136
The London Gazette, 104
The London Magazine, 109
Loudoun, Earl of, 63, 78–79, 82; quarrels with colonists, 161 (n. 40)
Louis XIV, King of France, 3
Lovejoy, Arthur O.: on the Great Chain of Being, 155 (n. 29)
Loyalists, American, 28
Luttrell, Temple, 113

Machiavelli: on survival of republics, 146
Magistrates: in Massachusetts, 6
Magna Carta: printed by Penn, 11
Maine, province of, 60
Manufacturers, interests of, 88

Index

Marvell, Andrew, 104

Maryland, 121; religious toleration in, 3, 5; early legislative divisions of, recorded, 119, 120, 124–25; publishes *Votes and Proceedings*, 124; demands record of votes in Continental Congress, 131–32

Massachusetts, 2, 3, 5, 6, 7, 9, 11, 13, 15, 21–23, 27, 33, 43, 48, 56, 61, 76, 78–79, 122; Charter of 1630, 4, 10, 16, 20, 49; Charter of 1691, 16, 53, 57, 58, 60, 76, 84, 120, 142; Act of Toleration resented in, 59; records proceedings of ratifying convention, 134; Explanatory Charter changes forms of government in, 142–43

Massachusetts General Court: laws of, 3, 20; and religion, 24; in quarrel over sloop, 33–34, 64; in quarrel with Shute, 57; and Explanatory Charter, 57–58, 120–21; salary issue, 60–61; constitution of, compared to England's, 61; powers of, extended, 62, 72; and land bank, 75, 77–78, 121, 122; compared to Parliament, 80; and quartering issue, 82; and Speaker, 120; divisions of, recorded, 120–24; prints *Journal*, 121; publishes *Votes*, 123; informs public of actions, 128; corruption of, charged, 129; erects gallery, 130–35; and controversy with Loudoun, 161 (n. 40)

Mather, Cotton, 18, 19, 160 (n. 20)

Mather, Increase, 8, 9–14, 15, 19–20, 48–51; his sermon on death of William III, 52–53

Matthew, Saint: quoted, 20

Mayhew, Jonathan, 29, 30

Mechanicks: economic demands of, 9; as artisans, 18

Media, xiii

Merchants, 9, 18, 75, 88

Militia Acts, 1

Miller, John, 112

Miller, Perry, 155 (n. 33)

Ministers: of religion in Massachusetts, 14, 16, 18, 24, 82; reconcile themselves to happiness, 146; and theological basis, 157 (n. 66). *See also* Clergy

Mist, Nathaniel, 108

Molasses Act, 46

Monarchy: English, restored, 1–3, 6; New England "not an enemy of," 14; limited character of, 28, 70; constituted real government, 66; of William III, 66–67; and cabinet, 69; when it needed Parliament, 71; consent of, required by Parliament, 160 (n. 22). *See also* Crown; *individual monarchs*

Money: paper, 19

Morgan, Dr. John, 36

Morris, Gouverneur: on dilemma of secrecy, 133

Morris, Lewis: his party, 27, 125, 128

Morris, Robert: on reporting of debates, 136, 149–50

Mutiny and Quartering Act, 82

Nature, human, 7

Navigation Acts, 14, 22, 44, 46, 59, 68, 70, 74, 81

Neale, Sir John, 92

Negroes: in revolt, 56

New England, 5, 6, 9, 10–15, 21, 26, 33, 49, 50, 51, 52, 53, 55, 60; Dominion of, 14, 45, 48, 143; crown's quarrel with, distracts from God's, 18; assembly powers, 72; feels safer, 79; continuity of its assemblies, 143; philosophical transformation of, 146

The New-England Courant, 121

New Jersey, 31

New light, 26

Index

Newton, Sir Isaac, 18; his mechanics as political theory, 67

New York, 11, 22, 27, 45, 83; land riots, 33; royal authority in, 51; books of laws begin in, 51; Leislerians, 51; anti-British grumbling in, 54; lawyers in, 55; and quartering, 82, 84; party politics of, 125; assembly records divisions, 125–26; controls printing, 125–26; records proceedings of ratifying convention, 134; press reports assembly debates of, 137

The New York Journal: reports assembly debates, 137

The New York Mercury, 126

The New-York Weekly Journal, 27

North, (Frederick), Lord, 40, 85, 112, 156 (n. 57); weakened by cumulative criticism, 135

North Carolina, 80

Notestein, Wallace, 96

Oakes, Urian, 8

Oliver (London alderman), 112

Onslow, Colonel George, 111

Onslowe, Richard: elected Speaker, 94

Order: on earth as in heaven, 7; natural, 8, 17, 18; Newtonian, 67

Otis, James, 23, 34, 35, 36, 79–80, 129

Palmer, John, 12, 13, 14

Park, William: prints *Maryland Gazette*, 124

Parker, Henry, 100

Parliament, xiv, 1, 2, 6, 10, 12, 22–23, 44, 70–78, 85, 87, 98, 115, 124; Long Parliament, 1, 104; sovereignty of, 35, 37, 38; Burke on, 39; and foundation of Georgia, 42; Cromwell's, 43; taxation by, 45–46; and colonial

government, 45, 46, 47–48, 51, 53, 59, 64, 76–77, 81–82; Convention Parliament of 1689, 46, 49, 67, 71, 80; authority of, questioned in colonies, 78–79; James Wilson on, 85–86; of 1571, 91; and renewed tension with crown, 104; Oxford Parliament 104; and national politics, 106; accountability of, 142; issue in American Revolution, 143; not called by Charles I, 144; longevity of, vs. triennial, 144; why it escaped reform in 18th century, 144–45; in imperial system, 145; supremacy of, affirmed by Otis, 157–58 (n. 69); power of, over colonial elections, 160 (n. 22), 163 (n. 32); bills against colonial charters in, 160 (n. 31); limits of, asserted, 164 (n. 50). *See also* House of Commons, House of Lords

Parsons, Philip, 95

Parties, 107

Passive obedience, 28, 29

Paternalism: outraged, British, 85

Paul, Saint: author of Romans, 30

Paxtons: march of, 33

Penn, William, 11, 16, 143

Pennsylvania: religious toleration in, 3, 5; prosperity in, 22; Paxton disorders in, 33; Assembly and quartering, 82; its *Journal*, 121; prints its proceedings as propaganda, 126–27; and quarrel with Denny, 126–27; and Dickinson-Galloway controversy, 128; continuity of, 143; debates Carey's petition, 149–50; constitution of, requires open doors, 150; records proceedings of ratifying convention, 134; Charter of 1701, 143

the People: element in politics, 17, 20, 25, 26, 28, 95, 96, 98, 102, 103,

Index

108; Otis on, 34; representation of, claimed by House of Commons, 90; supposed to have confided power to the Commons, 100; in changed relation to government, 140, 141

Perry, James: edits *Daily Gazetteer*, 113

Petition of Right, 96

Philadelphia, 83; prints for Maryland, 124; populous, 136; assembly debates reported in, 137

Philip: King Philip's war, 9

Piggott, Sir Christopher, 94

Pitt, William, Earl of Chatham, 35, 110

Place Bill, 108

Plantations. *See* Colonies

Pocock, J. G. A.: on American first principles, 143; on the owl of Minerva, 155 (n. 29)

Poland: peasants of, an example of slavery, 35; diet of, an example of anarchy, 71

Political State of Great Britain, 109

Politics, xv

Pope, Alexander, 36

Popery. *See* Roman Catholics

Population: growth of, 21, 80

Portland, Governor the Duke of, 74

Powell, Enoch, 94

Pownall, Governor Thomas, 161 (n. 40)

Prerogative. *See* Crown; *individual governors*

Prescott, Benjamin, 29, 83–84

Press: its liberty restricted in Massachusetts, 11; struggle for free, in New York, 27; parliamentary reporting by, 109–13; colonial, reports on Parliament, 134–35; silent on colonial assemblies, 135–36; reports on Congress, 139–40

Prince, Thomas, 60

Privy Council, 44, 48, 51, 57, 61, 68, 70, 91, 118, 120

Progress: idea of, 4

Property, 20, 27, 31, 65; confers rights, 6; Parliament represents, 144

Protestant religion: in England and France, 3; in New York, 11; churches affected by death of William III, 52

Public opinion, 115–16; under Charles I, 96–100; disaffection with Parliament, 101; concessions to American, by Congress, 132–33; British, misreported in colonies, 135

Pulteney, William: on parliamentary reporting, 110

Puritans, 6, 25, 43, 65; uphold godly commonwealth, 146

Purvis, John, 119

Putney Debates, 101

Pym, John: recalled by Americans, 65; speech of, published, 99

Quakers: hanged in Boston, 11; party in Pennsylvania, 127

Quebec, 19, 79

Randolph, Edward, 44

Rawson, Edward, 14, 15

Reed, Joseph, 36; identity discussed, 158 (n. 74)

Regulators, 33

Religion: declining observance of, in Massachusetts, 2; must be voluntary, 8; as cause of happiness, 20; and English government, 49; as test of loyalty, 95

Representation: political, xiv, 5, 113; of interests, 88; and communication, 89, 90; and legitimacy, 102; "whole nation" principle, 103–4, 106, 142; an

Index

THE AUTHOR

J. R. Pole has been Rhodes Professor of American History and Institutions at Oxford University since 1979. Before that Professor Pole was Reader in American History and Government and Vice-Master of Churchill College at Cambridge University, and for ten years previously, Lecturer in American History at University College, London. He has held appointments at Princeton University, the University of California, Berkeley, and the University of Chicago. His books include *Political Representation in England and the Origins of the American Republic*, *The Pursuit of Equality in American History*, and *Paths to the American Past*.